Doing Research with Children

ANNE GREIG
and
JAYNE TAYLOR

SAGE Publications
London · Thousand Oaks · New Delhi

First published 1999

SAGE Publications Ltd
6 Bonhill Street
London EC2A 4PU

SAGE Publications Inc.
2455 Teller Road
Thousand Oaks, California 91320

SAGE Publications India Pvt Ltd
32, M-Block Market
Greater Kailash – I
New Delhi 110 048

British Library Cataloguing in Publication data

A catalogue record for this book is available from the British Library

ISBN 0-7619-5589-5
ISBN 0-7619-5590-9 (pbk)

Library of Congress catalog card number 98-61371

Typeset by Type Study, Scarborough
Printed and bound in Great Britain by Athenaeum Press, Gateshead

For
James and Ellen,
and
Jayne's mother who died whilst we were writing the book

Contents

List of figures

List of boxes

List of tables

Acknowledgements

We are grateful for the support and encouragement of our colleagues in the School of Social Work, University of East Anglia and at University College Suffolk. Special thanks go to Julia Warner who provided first class assistance and without whom certain chapters would never have been produced. Thank you also to Lucy, Naomi and Jane at Sage for their remarkable patience, support and advice at every stage. Marian Brandon kindly allowed us to use some drawings from her research on maltreated children, and Sue Bailey provided her son Robert's drawings for comparison. Dawn Gregory wrote the Molly scenario for a workshop she co-presented with Anne, as well as providing vivacious friendship and a helpful dialogue of ideas.

PART I

THE SPECIAL NATURE OF CHILDREN IN RESEARCH – THEORIES AND APPROACHES

1 Introduction to research and children: a special relationship

Take two biologically similar children and rear them in different environments and they will most certainly differ in terms of their behaviour, their physique, their motivation and their achievements. Take two biologically different children and rear them together, giving them similar opportunities and experiences and they too will differ. It is these puzzling phenomena that have prompted scholars from the fields of psychology, biology, sociology, health and education to undertake research with child subjects in order to understand what makes children behave as they do. The body of knowledge built up over the last century has meant that we move towards the millennium with an amazing amount of insight into the minds and behaviours of the children that many of us work with every day. Those of us working in this era carry a great debt of gratitude to the painstaking work of those scholars who have spent their lives helping us to understand children better so that we may be more effective in our work.

This book is written with the clear intention of ensuring that the 1990s and beyond is not seen as a stagnant time in terms of research with children. The body of research that we have shows us that this is not an ill-founded intention. There have been many periods throughout the century where the acquisition of new knowledge seemed to be limited, whilst at other times knowledge acquisition gained an impetus which was staggering. A brief résumé of some of the major research themes will be discussed later in this chapter. Whilst it is important that we are grateful for the knowledge we have, we must, however, ensure that we are always moving forward, always searching and always pursuing greater understanding.

There are many, many ways of achieving new knowledge, but the key to this achievement, regardless of the field we work in, is training. We acknowledge that few of our readers will go on to make pure research their living, but we also recognise that professional people both during initial training and after qualifying need a sound knowledge of how to apply research and how to undertake research. This book is about applying research practically and undertaking research practically. It is essentially a practical book which is specifically designed for professionals who work, or intend to work, with children and who have to undertake research as part of their education or who need to undertake research, even on a very small scale, as part of their professional lives.

This book is also practical in that it recognises the reality of studying child subjects in the further pursuit of knowledge. Children do not exist in vacuums and their lives are naturally complex. They have to be if children are to arrive in adulthood with the repertoire of skills and behaviours which are essential for modern living. We have therefore taken an holistic perspective of the child and the child's environment, recognising that research training must be cognisant of the many variables which influence development and behaviour. We have drawn from the fields of psychology, sociology, biology, education and health in our discussions about research and in our considerations of the child subjects. We are explicit in our acknowledgement that children are special, and that research and research training which involves children, must also be special.

Not only are children special but they also hold a very special place in society. Whilst some of the research undertaken in pursuit of gaining understanding of children has been appalling in terms of what children have been expected to do and suffer, the majority of work has been undertaken sensitively and has followed correct ethical principles. We will focus on this theme in Chapter 8 but should give recognition in this opening section to the distinctive position which children hold in contemporary society. This has not always been the case, however, or at least that is the impression one is left with when studying historical perspectives of child care. As we will discuss later in the chapter, the child of today has rights which are universally held, widely adhered to and in most western societies are monitored by legislation.

Children are special

As we have briefly mentioned above, children are very special people. Defining what we mean by special is, however, a complex and difficult task. Perhaps what we mean is that children are different from the adults who control and describe the world as we know it. Perhaps it is because children are necessary for the survival of our species. Perhaps it is because children are an enigma – we don't understand so many things about them and they therefore puzzle us. Perhaps it is none or all of these things. What is evident is that children have, from biblical times to the present day, been singled out to varying extents as being exceptional beings who have afforded special consideration. Children are seen as an outward celebration of life, as the next generation and as the future of mankind. They also eventually grow and develop into adults, which perhaps gives us further insight into why they are considered special. The famous and infamous names from our history lessons at school were all once children themselves, which leads us to wonder why they developed in the way they did.

Special and very special

It is not the intention of this book to give a potted history of the place of children in society – there are many texts which adequately fulfil that aim. However, because we wish to focus upon doing research with children, we must spend a few moments looking at the child within our society so that we can explore the wider contexts of research.

People have children for a number of reasons which are not always easy to define. They are seen, by some, as desirable assets, as insurance to provide for them in their old age, as a sign of their fertility. Some religions dictate that the purpose of marriage is for the procreation of children, indeed in seventeenth century England childlessness was even considered to be a sin (Fraser 1984). Whatever the reason, on a macro level any society must ensure that it reproduces itself if it is to survive. On an individual level many cultures hold the expectation that adults will eventually marry and produce children. There are also those who have children because they do not believe in the use of, or have access to, reliable contraception.

Whether children are brought into the world by accident or by design, once born they have certain rights which are upheld by law. Children have the fundamental right to life, and before the abolition of capital punishment to deliberately take the life of a child was punishable by death. Today, whilst escaping the death penalty, child murderers can expect and receive the severest of punishment. Children also have the right to protection from harm and from neglect, they have the right to go to school and receive an education among other things. The Children Act (Department of Health 1989) and several charters, including the Universal Declaration of the Rights of the Child (UNICEF 1989), detail explicitly the rights of children as we will discuss in following chapters. Rights, however, only lay down the minimum expectations which society holds for its children. For the majority of parents and people within society, children are their future and they strive to ensure that the mistakes of one generation do not extend to the next. People generally want for children those things which they did not have themselves. They want children to have more opportunities, less hardship, more success and so on.

In order to ensure that children attain what society wishes for them, each generation must be analysed, evaluated and steps taken to rectify past mistakes. We must have understanding of children and how they develop, what factors adversely affect their progress and what factors will best promote their optimum development. Gaining this understanding is the driving force behind past, present and future research with children and crosses all professional boundaries. Geneticists, biologists, psychologists, educationists and sociologists have all striven for this greater understanding of children, albeit with differing philosophies, research traditions and methodologies.

If we accept the special status of all children within society we must also recognise that there are many children who, for a variety of reasons, must be considered to be very special. These children differ from their peers because, for example, they are exceptionally gifted or because of a physical or psychological dysfunction or because they are particularly vulnerable. These children have been, and are, the focus of a great deal of research activity which aims to discover why they are different, and the effects of their difference in terms of their present and future development. What we should emphasise here is that their rights and our responsibilities as researchers and professionals remain at least the same as for all children. In many cases, undertaking research with these very special children requires even greater training as we will discuss in the following section.

Special but not new

It is very easy for a new generation to fall into the trap of making assumptions about the past. Professionals will generally, as part of their training, study aspects of the history of their profession and will gasp in horror at how children were treated. Take for example, the past practice of separating sick children from their parents during hospitalisation because it was felt that parents upset children, or the punishment meted out to children in schools for the good of their 'moral' development. The important point to recognise here is that these things happened, not because those professionals did not view children as special but because they did. Our contemporaries of the past shared, without doubt, a similar aim to our own which was to care for children according to the former's training and/or apprenticeship. It is only when common practices are questioned that change occurs, otherwise the status quo will persist endlessly. We should not think ourselves superior in any way, for without doubt our own professional practices will be questioned in years to come. We can only ensure that we do our best to question all our practices and strive, as far as possible, to base our practice on sound research. This involves two different, but related notions. First, each professional has a responsibility to ensure that he or she is aware of current research, can intelligently interpret it and incorporate sound research into practice. This will be discussed fully in Chapter 4. Second, we should all constantly ask questions, and where there is a lack of research we should encourage investigation (see Chapter 2 for further discussion). This may mean undertaking research ourselves or enabling others to do so. However, such activity requires training, particularly when the research involves children, as we shall discover during the rest of this book, because as we have already said many times children are very special.

A final point to make about the past is that looking back does not always reveal the horror of past practice but can also make us realise that our predecessors had great insight into the needs of children – insight which appears sometimes to have been lost by some professions over the years. Froebel, the founding father of the *kindergarten* in the nineteenth century vividly illustrates this, for example, in his description of the first kindergarten:

> An institution for the fostering of human life, through the cultivation of the human instincts of activity, of investigation and of construction in the child as a member of the family, of the nation and of humanity; an institution for the self-instruction, self-education and self-cultivation of mankind, as well as for all-sided development of the individual through play, through creative self-activity and spontaneous self-instruction. (Froebel cited in Murray and Brown Smith 1922: 5)

Training for research

As all the professions move towards *all graduate* status, in the future all professionals who qualify should have undertaken some research training. This is seen by many as a positive benefit of raising the academic expectation of initial training programmes. There are those, however, who find the notion challenging, and one of the fears frequently raised is that graduate programmes lead to far too much small scale research being undertaken in practice areas by students. This is only one area of the wider debate which we will focus on in the following section.

The great majority of professions, perhaps with the exception of teaching, requires that those who enter will undergo generic training before specialising with children. Generic training aims to ensure a broad base of knowledge and in many instances gives the professional a 'taster' of work with a variety of groups, including different age groups. Research training has also tended to be generic with little consideration given to the differences between undertaking research with child or adult subjects. There are, however, very important differences. Children are not miniature adults nor, as we have already stated, do they generally exist in isolation. The social and emotional relationships of the child are stronger than at any other time of the lifespan and cannot be ignored. For example, studying the child in a laboratory situation without also studying the child in the naturalistic setting will limit the understanding gained (Dunn 1996). We will explore this further later on.

It is also important to differentiate between the study of children in general and the study of those children whom we have defined as very special. All children, for all sorts of reasons, are vulnerable, and this vulnerability is heightened in some children. These children are already in many ways often singled out because they are different, which is frequently what makes them attractive and interesting research subjects. Researchers who study these children do, however, require special skills so as not to accentuate differences overtly to the detriment of the particular child. The avoidance of harm necessitates particular skills in terms of understanding the nature of childhood, possessing knowledge about issues such as informed consent and, not least, being sensitive to differences. Schaffer (1990) discusses this point and questions past practices of focusing on negative aspects of differences. The current trend of moving away from investigating the negative effects of difference which some children exhibit, towards a focus upon the resilience of similar children, is a welcome development.

Research awareness versus research skills

Research training is a far broader concept than undertaking a small survey or experiment. We mentioned in our introduction that research training also involves applying research to our practice, and this is probably the more important skill. There is little point in belonging to a profession which has a sound research base if current research is not integrated into our practice. Take, for example, research which has recently been carried out into the operation of the child protection system in England (Child Protection Series 1995). This research series has highlighted many geographic anomalies within the system as well as areas of good practice, and each piece of research has made sound evidence-based recommendations for future practice. These recommendations have many, wide reaching implications for practice but, if implemented, should ensure a nation-wide system which does not disadvantage certain children and their families on the basis of where they happen to live. If the research is ignored and not acted upon, not only will a great deal of research time and money be wasted, but children and their families will continue to receive care which is less than they deserve.

In many instances, a profession's research base relies on experienced researchers, often located within university departments, undertaking research which produces recommendations which should then be put into place by practitioners. This is explored further in Chapter 4. The point is that both research skills and research awareness are needed, but for most practitioners it is the skill of being able to incorporate research into their practice which becomes paramount. Practice should be evidence based but the evidence does not need to be derived from personal research but from a wider knowledge of research which is being undertaken within, and outwith, a profession which can inform practice.

Small scale research – how valuable?

As we have mentioned above, there is concern about the volume of small scale research which is being undertaken generally (Department of Health 1993), and for those of us who focus upon children in our professional lives, this is a very important issue. Small scale research which is not communicated to the rest of our profession could lead to the duplication of effort, with the potential for many individuals investigating similar problems over and over again – the proverbial 'reinventing the wheel'. The continual re-investigation of a particular issue does not broaden a profession's knowledge base nor does it advance practice. There is also the potential for wasting valuable and often scarce resources.

There are times, however, when small scale research is appropriate and indeed where it is both desirable and valuable: for example, where a localised problem is identified or where a previous study has poor external validity (see Chapter 5) but the professional recognises that the findings may be applicable to their own practice. In this case it would certainly be of value to replicate a study to discover whether the findings are similar in a different setting. Recommendations can then be safely incorporated into practice because the evidence supports their incorporation.

There is also debate about what constitutes a small scale study. Traditionally, the 'smallness' related to the size of a particular sample, but in more recent years this view has been challenged. For example, a case study may focus on a single child or family but may be extremely complex in terms of what it proposes and very influential to practice. An early example is Axline's *Dibs: In Search of Self* (1964), which is a published study of one child's personality development through play therapy and provides a wealth of detail which can inform practice. Case studies are of immense value to the professions, particularly when they provide a wealth of detail and when a child perhaps portrays a rare behaviour. They may focus upon a single subject or a small sample but provide an excellent means of understanding complex phenomena (Yin 1994). We will discuss the case study in Chapter 6.

We should always be aware, however, that small scale research cannot generally replace studies conducted on a larger scale designed to lead to generalisable knowledge and recommendations.

Interprofessional research skills

We have mentioned above that research training with children should be different from training adults. A further complication is that the care of children is rarely a uniprofessional activity and yet there is a wide diversity of what professionals are taught and consequently a diversity of opinion about research. Research traditions tend to exist in most professions, ranging from the positivistic, deductive approaches favoured for example by doctors and pharmacists to the more qualitative, inductive approaches favoured by social scientists, many nurses and some teachers (see Chapter 3). If we are to take a truly holistic approach to caring for children and consequently researching with children, it is important that a more interprofessional approach is adopted. Not only do professionals in contemporary practice need to be aware of their own research traditions, they should also be skilled in recognising and valuing the research traditions of colleagues outwith their profession.

One of the greatest hurdles to overcome here is the rigid and hierarchical perspective which some professions hold in relation to methodologies. Yin (1994) discusses this issue and suggests that a more appropriate view of research methodologies is 'a pluralistic one' (p. 3). Different research strategies can be employed in different ways and rigidity only serves to hamper innovation. For example, case studies, according to Yin, can utilise exploratory, descriptive and explanatory strategies, just as experiments (traditionally seen as the only way of finding causal relationships) can have an exploratory motive. The important issue here is that where problems arise in practice relating to a child or a group of children, and research is undertaken, the process is, of course, important but so too is the outcome. At a 'grass roots' level it does not matter very much if one method or another is used as long as the process is rigorous and systematic, and the recommendations for changing practice (or not) are based upon sound, reliable and valid data (see Chapter 5 for further discussion).

There is also an issue about respecting the research traditions of particular professional groups which links back to Yin's pluralistic view (Yin 1994), which is of extreme importance in terms of moving research forward. Collaboration is something of a 'buzz word' both in contemporary practice and in research and is seen as desirable in that collaboration facilitates the holistic perspective for which we strive when working with children. Respect is about understanding and accepting that, whilst differences exist, this does not mean that one view is of a lesser value than another. It is very easy to take an egocentric view of the world and to use our own professional background as a reason for being critical of others. We have anecdotal examples of both stances where nursing students have submitted work to different Local Research Ethics Committees (see Chapter 8) which tend to be medically dominated in terms of membership. One committee responds positively to proposals which take a qualitative stance, recognising that this type of approach is different from the usual proposals which they receive. Occasionally, clarification of the methodology is required but there is certainly respect for work of this nature. A second committee frequently responds with comments such as 'this is not research' or 'this is audit' when clearly it is not. An ethics committee has in the past refused permission for a qualitative study to proceed, on the basis that no questionnaire was submitted, although the study aimed to use participant observation for data collection!

There is, however, light at the end of the tunnel. More and more educational programmes are incorporating shared learning into the curricula, particularly during initial training programmes but also at Masters level and beyond. Child protection training has been at the forefront of this development facilitated by the *Area Child Protection Committees* and their multidisciplinary training subgroups, set up under legislation emanating from the Children Act (Department of Health 1989). This not only promotes respect but also leads to a greater understanding of different perspectives. This type of interprofessional education is about the identification of barriers to collaboration and ways of overcoming such barriers. Such interprofessional education is increasingly evident in research training and is a welcome initiative.

Major research themes

As we have already discussed, it is important for members of a profession to undertake research to keep a profession moving forward and to advance practice which is based upon evidence. In some ways the barriers and rivalry which traditionally existed between some professions might well have aided progression albeit in a covert way. Each profession has its pride and none would wish to be viewed as being backwards or accused of halting progress. There has been evidence of where this type of scenario has occurred in the past, and the effects have been notable (see Taylor and Woods 1997), as we will discuss in the next section.

What is evident, however, is that because of the complex nature of childhood it is inevitable that research undertaken by one profession relating to an aspect of childhood will impact upon the practice of another profession, or indeed several other professions. Resistance and closing of the ranks (a response which has been observed in the past) does not help the child, the family or the wider society and ultimately does not help the professionals themselves. It can lead to stagnation within a profession and may be one reason why there have been times in the past when professions have appeared not to increase, or build upon, existing knowledge bases. It is hoped that with a greater emphasis on shared learning and training, and greater collaboration in research and practice, that we will not in future observe instances of professional resistance to change which is detrimental to the child.

At the very beginning of this chapter we referred to perceived peaks and troughs of advancing knowledge in relation to children, and we can only really guess at why this occurred. The professional resistance mentioned above might be one answer. When a profession becomes insular it seldom advances. Inward conflict leads to energies being used to resolve inner conflict and research becomes less of a priority. It is also probably true that when a society becomes insular or experiences conflict the same thing happens. The last century has seen periods of war, economic depression and recession, large scale epidemics and political changes which have certainly influenced the forward momentum of research activity. Without doubt, conflict within a society impacts upon the activities of professions and it becomes difficult to decipher responsibility for stagnation in research, or indeed progression. Suffice to say that research activity appears to mirror the concerns of professions and society, and rightly so. Research is about solving real problems and the major research themes of the last century can be seen to relate to changes which have occurred within society. We explore some of these themes in the next section. Clearly we could not begin to cover all such themes and can only offer a few exemplars to illustrate the preceding discussion. These exemplars focus upon two areas. First, how research is generated by the concerns of a society and second, how research undertaken by one profession impacts on others.

Learning

One of the major areas of research which has spanned the last century is learning. Researchers have sought to discover, from a variety of perspectives how children learn, and the knowledge gained from such research has influenced virtually all, if not all, professionals who work with children. Much of the early work on learning was restricted to animal studies: for example, Pavlov's work with dogs which was instrumental in defining the learning process which is referred to as *classical conditioning* (Pavlov 1927), Thorndike's work with cats (see Buskist and Gerbing 1990) during which he discovered the *Law of Effect*, and Skinner's work with pigeons and rats (Skinner 1938) which defined the learning process referred to as *operant conditioning*. The application of these theories to human learning, and to learning in children in particular, was notable, and the work of these early researchers formed the basis of further research into human learning and human personality. Albert Bandura (1977) , for example, utilised Skinner's theories about behavioural consequences and blended them with his own ideas producing the theory (along with others) of *social learning* (a detailed account of this and other cognitive theories can be found in Chapter 2).

The work undertaken on the psychology of learning has had much wider application and has led to the advancement of practice in other professions concerned with the care of children. Sociologists have borrowed these theories: for example, Eppel and Eppel (1966) looked at the influence of early learning upon later moral behaviour. Educationists have also utilised learning theories (as one would expect) to inform classroom activities (Panton 1945; Child 1986), and health care professionals, particularly those involved with health promotion activities with children (Taylor and Müller 1995; Taylor 1996), have borrowed such theories to underpin their work.

Clearly then the impact of one profession's work has had a major impact on the practice of others. What is also interesting is to note that the impetus for much of this work came before, between and after the two World Wars. It is also interesting to speculate as to why learning became, and remains, so high on the research agenda. The lack of evidence in this area leads us to speculation, and we don't pretend to have any or all of the answers. Perhaps the pioneering work in Germany by Froebel (see Woods 1997) led to some action by educationists, perhaps academic comparisons with other developed countries prompted the need to ensure that our children did not fall behind, or perhaps concern about the moral behaviour of adolescents was the prompt. The list of possibilities is endless.

Adolescent deviance, delinquency and morality

The moral values and standards of adolescents has long been a subject which has fascinated researchers and is the second major theme upon which we focus. Concern was evident for a very long time before the 1950s and 1960s, but it was during these two decades that it became an explosive subject and the focus of a great deal of research. There was much speculation as to whether deviance and delinquency were attributable to genetic or environmental influences, or a combination of both, and particular emphasis was placed upon increasing understanding of the effect of early environmental variables upon later delinquent behaviour (this is a fine example of what Schaffer (1990) described as focusing upon those who showed abnormal behaviour rather than focusing on those who showed normal behaviour).

Again, because of a lack of evidence we are left to speculate as to why there was such a spurt of activity in this field during these decades. The origins of activity probably lie in the interest in a group of young people who had been born during, or just after, the war years and who were in their adolescence during the 'flower power' era with its perceived association with sexual freedom, illicit drug taking and a greater questioning by young people of traditional and cultural practices. What we saw here was perhaps a society trying and needing to find a cause for adolescent behaviour in the sixties because the behaviour was so alien to them. Or perhaps society needed to find some answers because it wished to be absolved of any guilt on its own part in what was seen as declining adolescent morals. How much more comfortable it feels to be able to blame the birth control pill, or television, or drugs or alcohol, or the 'pop' music scene, than to attribute blame to ourselves.

Whatever the reasons, as we have already stated, research into this area took on an incredible impetus which influenced sociologists, psychologists and educationists, and had a major influence upon professional practice at the time. The publication of many studies in paperback form, and adapted for general reading, also influenced media and public opinion. Notable studies included a study of the moral values and dilemmas of adolescents (Eppel and Eppel 1966), a study called *The Unattached* (Morse 1965) involving three social workers working for three years with young people who had experienced varying degrees of family breakdown, Eysenck's study of *Crime and Personality* (1964), and Storr's exploration of the effects of childhood upon later perverse or deviant sexual behaviour (Storr 1964). There were many, many more.

Children's relationships

A third major research theme which deserves our attention relates to the relationships which children have with their parents, in particular, and the effects of 'unusual' relationships upon child development. This theme had been apparent in literature earlier in the century but became high on the agenda after Bowlby (1951) made his bold claims about the importance of early caring relationships to the ability to love in later life (a detailed account of this and other theories of emotion and relationships can be found in Chapter 2). Bowlby's work was extremely influential and as a result of his work a World Health Organisation Expert Committee (1951) declared that if day nurseries and crèches were allowed to proliferate then permanent damage would be caused to the emotional development of the future generation.

We have, in the last two sections hypothesised as to the impetus for research and would wish to do so in this section. It is not very difficult. The economic climate following the Second World War was such that politically it was desirable to encourage women back into the homes so that men returning from the war could find employment in jobs which had, during the war years, been undertaken by women.

In the years that followed Bowlby's publication a great deal of research has been undertaken which has sought to either confirm or dispute Bowlby's claims. Such works include studies by Ainsworth et al. (1978) into secure and insecure attachment, Newson and Newson's work (1963) into patterns of infant care, Stern's work (1977) on the infant and mother relationship and Robertson's work (see Robertson and Robertson 1989) on separation.

The work in this field did not, however, end there. The nursing profession at first ignored the work undertaken by psychologists which was critical of the practice of separating sick children from their parents. The publication of studies by Douglas (1975) and Hawthorn (1974) highlighted the immediate and potential long term effects of separation, and the inception of the *National Association for the Welfare of Sick Children in Hospital* (NAWCH which later became *Action for Sick Children*) led eventually to a structured campaign to change practices within hospitals. It was, however, several years after the publications of these studies that practices changed on a large scale.

Work in this field was also transmuted in the last two decades to focus upon the effects of divorce on children and the effects of living in one-parent families and reconstituted families. Such studies, including those by Hetherington et al. (1979, 1985), Guidubaldi et al. (1986) and Kulka and Weingarten (1979) highlighted important variables which influence how children are affected by different situations and it is difficult to draw generalisable conclusions. Clearly, however, this is another example of how research has mirrored the issues of contemporary society – the divorce rate increase correlates positively with the amount of research activity in the field.

Child health and illness

The last major theme which we will focus on relates to child health and the research which has been undertaken in this field. There has always been concern about the health and well-being of children, and assumptions are wrongly made that in the past people had large families, expecting some of their children to die, and therefore the death of a child did not, somehow, matter. Death and illness did matter very much and that 163 children in every thousand still died before their first birthday at the turn of the century means that there are still many elderly people alive who can attest to the pain caused by the death of a sibling. Infectious diseases, such as tuberculosis, cholera, typhoid and diphtheria were rife at the time and spread through communities, often killing several members of a family within days or weeks of each other.

Over the last century a great deal of progress has been made. The discovery of antibiotics and the introduction of wide scale immunisation, as well as the inception of the National Health Service in 1948 has had a huge impact upon mortality and morbidity in childhood. Yet, research in this field is again typical of the concerns of society. Whilst children were dying of infectious diseases the focus of research was on a cure and prevention. In the late 1980s and early 1990s the major cause of infant mortality was sudden infant death, and researchers turned the focus of their attention to this field. As a result of research (see CESDI 1994) practices of child care have changed, including laying babies on their backs to sleep, placing their feet near the foot of the cot to prevent them

sliding down the bed, recommendations about optimum room tempera-
tures and recommendations about not smoking near babies.

A further area of research which can be seen to be a direct response to
societal issues in child care relates to children and families with Human
Immunodeficiency Virus (HIV) and Acquired Immunodeficiency Syndrome (AIDS) related conditions. When it first became apparent that
children were being infected and affected by HIV, particularly those
who had been infected by the receipt of contaminated blood and blood
products, research tended to focus upon rates of infections (Prose 1990;
Husson et al. 1990). Later research has focused much more on the prevention of infection and upon therapeutic approaches to infected and
affected children (see Stine 1997). Research has not only been confined to
doctors undertaking medical research but has widened its focus to
include those from psychology, sociology and education who have
added further to the body of knowledge within their own professions
and to the professions of others, by studying the effects of HIV and AIDS
from a wide variety of stances.

Child health is our last brief example of an area of research activity,
and as we stated at the beginning of this section, it is impossible to do
justice to all areas of research with children, nor do we attempt to do so.
The intention of these examples is to look at how research is steered and
to highlight how research is, and should be, reactive to society's problems. We have also set out to give examples of how research in one area
will impact upon other areas, leading to a cascade of research which
focuses upon a similar topic but which has its own peculiar approach
and perspective.

Conclusion

Research is, then, vital to the health of a profession and likewise reflects
the health of a profession. Professions can stagnate and fail to increase or
build upon existing knowledge bases as we have seen throughout the last
decades. At other times, however, a particular research theme has
emerged from society and has captured its imagination. At these times
researchers from many professions will, individually or in collaboration,
focus on different aspects of the same topic. When this happens real
progress is made.

Research is not only vital for the health of a profession but is also
essential for the client group the profession serves – in this case children
and their families. The rest of this book is about the importance of research for the good of our chosen client group, who are special people
and who deserve special consideration.

2 Theory for research and practice with children

- *Situation 1.* A mother, having watched a controversial chat show, asks a nursery teacher if she should withdraw her child from day care and give up work because she now believes that children of working mothers suffer and that a group care setting is not as good as being at home with mother. What should the nursery teacher do and say to this mother?
- *Situation 2.* A nurse is concerned about the possible effects and potential damage to families in which there is a child with a long term illness requiring frequent and intensive separations between the child and the family. Is there anything the nurse can do to better understand the process and at the same time provide support for the families?
- *Situation 3.* Following the publication of a story in a popular woman's magazine, the help-line of a fostering and adoption support group is besieged with callers seeking advice on the value of cultivating a relationship between an adopted child and the biological mother. What can these callers be reasonably told?

The child care practitioner or researcher is not alone in improving her personal understanding and in making important decisions on complex issues like these. For each practice situation described above, there exists an established knowledge base of related theory and research. This knowledge is there to inform and guide those who work or research in the field of child care and development. For instance, there is a great deal known about child–carer attachments, separation and loss. There is a lot known about the relative contributions of home-day-care and parent-teacher to child education. Some of these questions are not, however, so well represented in theory and research as others. Relatively little is known about fathers in general and single parents in particular. Not much is known about the costs and benefits of maintaining relationships between an adopted child and the biological mother. This does not mean that there is no role for theory in these cases. On the contrary, existing theories in related areas can be adapted or new theories created and this will guide and generate much needed research in important but neglected areas. Nevertheless, the mere mention of the word 'theory' can drive terror into the hearts of research students and practitioners alike. The former because of the overwhelming range of possible and often complex theories which they are only beginning to touch upon in lectures, and the latter because they have come to rely upon their practice experience or intuition and may feel threatened that the knowledge they have is no longer valued. For those of us who teach about the role of theory in research and practice, it is apparent that, in the undergraduate population and even beyond into the classrooms, wards and homes, that 'theory' can be regarded as a dirty word. In this chapter, it is hoped to show that the nature of theory is, in fact, rather like that of a valuable, important and useful friend. The undergraduate needs to realise that a sound grasp of theory – like all good friendships – needs to be worked on and developed over time. The intuitive practitioner need not feel insecure, because experience creates an advantage in being able to recognise and use theory effectively. We all need to appreciate that theory is not a mystical thing visited upon us by superior beings, but is instead an ordinary part of everyday thinking and being human.

The fact is that theorising is a natural, human compulsion that helps us to organise our perceptions of the world and therefore make it easier to predict and control. For instance, a parent who notices withdrawn behaviour and school refusal in her 8 year old child is confronted by an unpredictable situation which disrupts routine and which poses a threat to longer term adjustment and security. Finding the reason why the behaviour has appeared, describing it, explaining it, predicting it and controlling it is a matter of survival. Theories have been described as nets cast to catch what we call 'the world', to rationalise, to explain, and to master it. In the world of child development, you may have a theory that the 8 year old has a behavioural disorder because of an underlying problem in the child's relationship with the mother. You will then investigate the nature of this relationship to describe what is wrong and to implement changes. Or you may have the theory that the child's behaviour disorder is simply a matter of an ineffective parental regime of rewards and punishments. You will then describe that regime, explain the problems, predict patterns and bring about changes which will control or alter the behaviour. As both these examples suggest, theory can be viewed as a stage upon which observations and experiments can be conducted and serve an important practical function by guiding research and practice.

Why do people who work with children need theory?

Every individual who deals with children has this very human need to make sense of them. If little Ben is creating mayhem in his reception class, foster placement or medical ward, the urge to observe his behaviour, describe what he is doing, find both explanations and solutions is essential. The explanations generated can help predict not only Ben's behaviour but may also be generalised to other similar children and situations. Ultimately, it should be possible to understand or predict and to devise a means of controlling, preventing or curing such behaviour. These processes of describing, explaining, predicting and controlling are the very essence of theory, and professionals in child education, health and welfare need to do all of these things on a daily basis. In many cases, far reaching decisions about a child's future will have to be made on the basis of such theorising. A sound understanding of theory is therefore of the utmost importance. There are, however, many different theoretical perspectives in child development, many different ways of 'seeing' the world and, consequently, many different explanations and solutions for any one given situation. For example, a mother seeking advice on the disruptive behaviour of her child could, potentially, receive diverse and incompatible explanations and solutions depending on which professional is consulted. An educational psychologist may theorise that a learning disability is underlying the disruptive behaviour and recommend special tuition or removal to a special school depending on severity. A health visitor may theorise that food intolerance often underlies child behaviour disorders and refer the child to a dietician. A social worker may theorise that social hardship and inadequate parenting are the source of the behaviour problem and implement a programme of parenting skills and social support or removal of the child from the parent into residential care. Professional theoretical perspectives can therefore have a massive impact leading to a range of possible futures for a given child, ranging from labelling and exclusion from mainstream education to the gradual entry into the criminal justice system. Whilst this may be an extreme example, it is an important one because it is where concerns within and across different professions diverge, that no man's land in between, where children are most at risk of long term damage or even brushes with death. As we mentioned in Chapter 1, seeking to improve the ways in which different professional groups can understand the theories and practices of each other and work together in the interests of children is a goal which will take us well into the 21st century (Pugh et al. 1994). Finally, another reason why people who work with children need theory is because much of the policies and legislation which dictate the roles, practices and rights of both practitioner and child, are formulated on the basis of various established bodies of theoretical knowledge. According to the Guidance on the 1989 Children Act (HMSO 1990), the implicit child care principles have been developed over a long period and have many roots, including knowledge from child development, psychology, psychiatry and sociology. The importance of understanding the nature of these underlying theories is obvious. It will lead to a better understanding of the nature of the job to be done as well as the nature of children.

Theories for guiding and interpreting research and practice with children

In doing research with children we are fortunate to have so many theories to choose from: Psychoanalytic Theory; Ethological Theory; Learning Theory; Cognitive-Developmental Theory and Ecological Theory. The popularity of these theories owes much to their ability to inform us about the child in interaction with the environment either as originally formulated or as they have been revised by subsequent theorists.

Psychoanalytic theories

The founding father of psychoanalytic methods and theory was Freud (1901, 1905, 1923). Freud trained as a physician, specialising in the study of the nervous system. In treating his patients, he noticed that some had illnesses for which no biological cause could be found, such as the mental illnesses of hysteria, anxiety and phobia. He was inclined to cure these patients by listening to them talking freely and without interruption about their current thoughts, feelings and desires. Freud's aim during this clinical procedure was to understand the underlying processes of the patient's mind and personality and also to provide a 'talking cure'. These clinical experiences resulted in Freud's formulation of a theory on the origins and development of the personality and its disorders. Freud believed that adult mental illness originated in childhood and that in analysing what went wrong, it would be possible to better understand the process of normal personality development.

According to psychoanalytic theory, the psychological system and its development is best described in 3 ways: it is dynamic, structural and sequential. *Dynamic* refers to Freud's conceptualisation of the human mind as driven, as machines are, by energy; *structural* refers to Freud's mapping of the mind into the id, the ego and the superego – 3 separate structures which work together in order to 'balance' the dynamic energy; and *sequential* refers to Freud's belief that as the body and its neurological awareness progresses, sequentially, through a systematic focus on one erogenous zone after the other, there will be a parallel progression through various psychological stages related to these erogenous zones and which will be manifested in personality. The personality stages corresponding to stages in neurological stages are oral, anal, phallic, latent and genital. These are described in more detail in the next section. Salkind (1985) describes these dynamic structural and sequential concepts as components which overlap and are interrelated. Figure 2.1 depicts Freud's conceptualisation of the psychological system. The overlaps and interrelations are important: for example the dynamic energy is unconscious and played out between the id, the ego and the superego, which are also sequential and subject to varying degrees of unconsciousness.

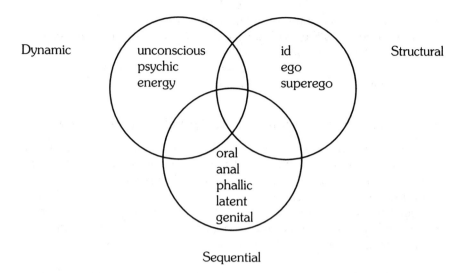

Figure 2.1   *Freud's psychological system*

Source: Adapted from Salkind, N.J. (1985) *Theories of Human Development*, p. 89.
Copyright John Wiley and Sons, Inc., 1981, 1985. Reproduced with permission

The dynamics of the psychological system

Just as machines are driven by energy, the human psychological system is driven by *psychic energy* which is biologically based. Psychic energy is unconscious and comes from instincts, the purpose of which is to promote survival of the species and of the individual. The most powerful energy drive is that which serves the procreation of the species – the sexual instinct – which Freud called *Eros*, and the special form of energy needed to maintain its development is called *libido*. Other drives identified are life-preserving for the individual such as the avoidance of hunger and pain, and *Thanatos*, the drive representing aggression and death. As with other forms of energy, biological drives like these are subject to tension, depending on the balance between biological needs, developmental demands and environmental support and hindrances. The psychological equivalent of this tension is *anxiety*.

The structure of the psychological system

At birth, the psychological system is all *id* (Latin for 'that thing'), the part of the psyche that seeks instant gratification of the instinctual drives. The id has free reign until the child is aged 2 and becomes more mobile. At this time, the child is likely to be denied instant gratification indirectly, and the child develops *unconscious* coping strategies to deal with the resulting anxiety. These strategies may include *defence mechanisms* such as denial, repression and projection. This phase also sees the creation of the *ego* which becomes the thinking part of the psyche and which plays an important role in the resolution of the conflicts that arise between the drive for instant gratification and the reality imposed by caregivers. By the school years the infant has also developed a *superego*. This represents parental standards which the child has internalised.

The sequential development of the psychological system

Not only is the structure of personality developed over time and as a result of interaction between instinctual drives and responses from caregivers, this development also is closely linked to discrete *stages* of physical–neurological development. In Freud's view, as the child's nervous system develops through various stages of sensual or sexual awareness there would be a related psychosexual progression in the development of the personality. Freud identified five sequential psychosexual stages:

1 The Oral Stage (0–1 year). At birth the child's neurological pleasure centre is focused on the mouth. Oral behaviours such as sucking and biting are the child's pleasure source.
2 The Anal Stage (1–3 years). As the child's body develops, neurological awareness of the anus is in place. Elimination and retention of faeces are a source of pleasure at the same time when the child is being toilet trained.
3 The Phallic Stage (3–5 years). At this time there is increased sensitivity in the genital area, and both sexes are likely to find pleasure in the exploration of the genital area, and children become unconsciously sexually attracted to the parent of the opposite sex. This is called the *Oedipus Complex* in boys and the *Electra Complex* in girls. These complexes are characterised by the rivalry with the same-sex parent for the sexual attention of the opposite-sex parent, a fear of the same-sex parent, and an attempt to deal with the resulting anxiety through the defence mechanism of *identification* with their rival.
4 The Latency Stage (5–12 years). At this time, sexual impulses are not an issue. It is a period of resolution following the anxiety of the pre-school years. Identification with same-sex peers is a feature at this stage, and sexual impulses, in whichever form they have been resolved, will remain latent, hidden until the challenges of puberty.
5 The Genital Stage (12–18 years, plus). Sexual impulses resurface with the onslaught of hormonal activity and genital regrowth which accompanies puberty. During adolescence, the child should reach a mature form of heterosexual love.

In summary then, personality development is a stage-like process with basic tasks or needs which are focused upon during each stage. The child has to move through each stage resolving tensions in the best way that she can. The success a child has at each stage is heavily dependent on interactions with caregivers. If the child fails to resolve tensions and successfully achieve developmental tasks, then evidence of 'fixation' at these unsuccessfully resolved stages will be evident in their adult personality. Individual personality, then, is a result of the degree of success and support the child has had in traversing these psychosexual stages.

Erikson (1963, 1980) shares many of Freud's basic assumptions on the nature of personality and its development. The three most important differences are Erikson's emphasis on the social and cultural influence on personality rather than the biological and sexual maturation; his emphasis on a cognitive drive for identity; and a lifespan developmental approach. Erikson proposed eight psychosocial stages of development, each of which is represented by psychosocial tasks or 'dilemmas'.

1 Basic Trust or Mistrust (0–1 year). In the first year of life the child needs to develop a sense of predictability in the world in which he lives and a sense of his ability to influence people and events which feature in his life. A sensitive and responsive caregiver is crucial in helping the child resolve these tasks successfully so that he learns to trust and carry this trust with him into other relationships and situations.
2 Autonomy or Shame and Doubt (2–3 years). As the toddler begins to move around independently, he needs careful guidance and support with failures. Otherwise, the child will develop self-doubt and shame.
3 Initiative or Guilt (4–5 years). The child is trying out new cognitive strategies in his attempts to explore the world around him. Frustration and aggression are common, and the child is highly active. Caregivers may over-restrict or punish the child, which will inhibit his initiative and lead to a sense of guilt.
4 Industry or Inferiority (6–12 years). As the child goes to school, there is a basic need for a sense of competence in skills which are valued by adults and peers. A failure to do so will lead to feelings of inferiority.
5 Identity or Role Confusion (13–18 years). The task of puberty and adolescence is to develop a sense of sexual and occupational identity. At the end of this stage, the individual should have an integrated sense of self.
6 Intimacy or Isolation (19–25 years). In early adulthood, sexual maturity enables the successful attainment of intimate relationships.
7 Generativity or Stagnation (26–40 years). In middle adulthood, the task is generativity, usually through childrearing or other creative achievements.
8 Ego Identity or Despair (41 years plus). The task of late adulthood is the ability to look back on achievements and experiences with a sense of pride and acceptance, which leads to ego integrity. Failure to do this will lead to anger, disappointment and despair.

At all stages in early childhood, there is a need to experience some mistrust, doubt, guilt and failure as it is adaptive to do so. Table 2.1

Table 2.1 A comparison between Freud's psychosexual stages of personality development and Erikson's psychosocial stages of personality development

Era of development	Freud's psychosexual stage	If fixated	Effect on personality	Erikson's psychosocial stage	Task failure	Effect on personality
Maturity	–	–	–	Ego integrity	↑	Despair, anger
Adulthood	–	–	–	Generativity	↑	Stagnation
Young Adulthood	–	–	–	Intimacy	↑	Isolation
Adolescence	Genital	↑	Sexual and social immaturity	Identity	↑	Role confusion
Middle Childhood	Latency	↑	No fixation	Industry	↑	Inferiority
Early Childhood	Phallic	↑	Overly reckless or opposite	Initiative	↑	Guilt
Toddlerhood	Anal	↑	Overly tidy, obstinate or opposite	Autonomy	↑	Doubt/shame
Infancy	Oral	↑	Oral behaviour, e.g. smoking, overeating, passive	Trust	↑	Mistrust

Source: Adapted from Berndt, T.J. (1997) Child Development, p 22. Copyright Times Higher Education Group, Inc., 1997. Reproduced with permission

illustrates the psychosocial stages of Erikson together with the psycho-sexual stages of Freud and indicates the effect on personality when a developmental task fails.

Psychoanalytic theory is a good theory in that it has inspired various revised versions and is drawn on in child play therapy with severely emotionally disturbed children. Other important theories share its assumptions about the importance of early childhood experiences and relationships, especially with primary caregivers. It is also valued for explaining emotional behaviour and development and for showing the sequential qaulitatively changing nature of the developmental tasks facing children at different ages. It is an attractive theory, full of bright metaphors. Unfortunately, this also leads to lack of clarity of constructs and some inconsistency, for example applying castration anxiety to little girls as well as boys! Such features make it a difficult theory to test.

Ethological theory

Ethology is the study of behaviours that are rooted in our evolutionary past, so in order to understand what ethologists do and how they view child behaviour, it is necessary, first, to understand the theory of evol-ution itself. According to Darwin (1859), all living organisms on the planet evolved from a few common ancestors and evolution is the com-plex process through which organisms change in response to the pres-sures that are placed on them by a variable, unstable environment. Darwin's extensive observations of various species on the Galapagos Islands convinced him that all living creatures produce more offspring than can survive and so they must compete in their natural habitats by way of adaptation for the varying resources and sustenance. The natural order is that those who can't adapt will die, and those who do will survive, reproduce and pass on their characteristics into the gene pool and into the next generation. This explains how homo sapiens 'evolved' the characteristic of upright posture. In other words, organisms vary through reproduction, each generation resulting in new combinations of genetic material.

In studying behaviour, ethologists assume that behaviours are like biological characteristics. Just as the structure of the body progresses through subtle variation in the gene code, so are certain classes of be-haviour. These behaviours are universal within a given species and are instinctive or genetically programmed. The basic function of these innate behaviours is to promote the survival of the species. Ethologists have identified three kinds of instinctive behaviours: reflexes, taxes and fixed action patterns. Reflexes include sucking, grasping and walking. Taxes are locomotor responses which facilitate protection and nurturance, such as cuddling, and fixed action patterns are programmed sequences of co-ordinated actions which can be very complex in humans, for example

nurturing routines and protective responses towards infants. These behaviour patterns only usually manifest in the presence of certain significant or 'signed stimuli' in the environment. For instance, in geese, the
presence of a mobile object results in the 'follow' behaviour pattern which
facilitates bonding. In humans, a mother disappearing from view may
elicit a distress response from the infant. A sudden piercing cry from a
babbling child will trigger a parental 'pattern of caring'. Ethologists believe that there are many signed stimuli and fixed action patterns which
function to ensure the care and protection of the infant and ultimately the
survival of the species. Consider how adult humans readily respond to
any child in distress, adopt the young of others, respond to baby features
of the young of any species and the way that babies smile, reeling adults
in and eliciting positive responses such as baby talk or motherese. One of
the consequences of these interdependent chains of stimuli and responses
is that the child forms a specific attachment to a particular caregiver,
usually the mother. This notion has stimulated some of the most exciting
research ever done with children. John Bowlby (1907–90) was a brilliant
psychiatrist who applied psychoanalytic theory to his earlier writings on
the mother–child relationship, particularly the view that the earliest
relationships were crucially important for longer term development and
adjustment. However, after discovering ethology, he believed that ethological principles better explain the nature of the child's tie to his mother –
that is, the complex, interdependent repertoire of instinctive behaviours
in both infant and parent which function to create proximity between the
child and caregiver and lead to the creation of a bond. However, as the
child has to learn who his mother is and what kind of mother she is, and
the mother needs to adapt to her infant, conditions exist in which an
infant and mother can fail to bond or bond in a maladaptive way. An
attachment is an emotional bond in which the person feels secure and the
other person is a safe base from which to explore the world around. There
are far-reaching implications for this theory (see Chapter 6 for a summary
of attachment research and classification procedures). Before we do consider practical implications of psychoanalytic and ethological theories,
let's consider very briefly some of the findings of relevant research.

Early researchers on institutionally reared children typically held the
view that a good mother–child relationship was crucial for normal
healthy development and that these children would display the developmental consequences of maternal deprivation. These early studies did
indeed show that institutionalised children were mentally retarded,
socially maladjusted and suffered poor health and high mortality rates.
In general they could be unresponsive to adults. In a longitudinal study of
institutionally reared 4 year olds (Tizard and Hodges 1978; Tizard and
Rees 1975) it was found that the same children who at 8 years had been
either returned to their parents or adopted, usually achieved normal IQ
scores yet still displayed a range of social adjustment problems such as
disobedience, unpopularity and attention seeking. Even children who did

get responsive caregivers still struggled in forming relationships because, by age 4, children could have had more than fifty carers! Ethological studies on infant monkeys were also strongly indicating the importance of the infant's early social environment. Laboratory studies on monkeys reared in social isolation from birth until 1 year old, ate well and grew normally but behaved bizarrely. When reintroduced to other monkeys, they were often overly aggressive or cowered and showed abnormal sexual behaviour. Females who did manage to mate successfully were poor mothers, neglecting and abusing their offspring. If the isolation period extended beyond 6 months, it was impossible to rehabilitate the socially deprived monkeys (Harlow and Mears 1979). However, if the monkeys were gradually reintroduced to social situations, placing it first with a younger monkey, the isolate monkey gradually learned to interact with older monkeys in an adaptive way, despite its early deprivation (Novak and Harlow 1975). Also on a positive note, Schaffer and Emerson (1964) found that human infants, by 18 months of age, have formed multiple close attachments to a number of other responsive individuals in their social environment. In fact, only 18% of infants studied had only one close attachment. The importance of siblings (Dunn 1985) and peers (Rubin et al. 1990) have also been studied, and like other important social relationships, these are highly supportive when they work well but can also be dysfunctional when they don't. Studies of this kind highlight the importance of early social and physical environment in fostering security, love and exploration. They remind us that the child is always in partnership with others such as parents, carers, siblings and peers. The child is affected by them but also has an impact on them. The key for healthy development appears to be the presence of responsive caregivers.

Practical implications of psychoanalytic and ethological theories for researchers and practitioners

1 *The interdependent nature of social relationships and their requirement for mutual adaptation.* In addressing the needs or nature of a child, we need to consider the broader social environment. Failure to treat one may be a failure to treat either. Parents, children and others can be involved in child-centred practice.
2 *The importance of early childhood experiences of both social and physical environment.* Caregivers need to provide a sensitive and responsive type of provision which takes full account of the individual child's needs for experience and stimulation. Environments and relationships should be secure and provide opportunities for the child to play and explore. When dealing with parents, it may be necessary to explore the nature of their own early childhood experiences.
3 *The importance of special and multiple attachments.* In providing care for children it is essential for one individual to get to know the child in detail in order to provide more sensitive and appropriate responses.

Meanwhile, the benefits of involvement with friends, siblings, parents and other adults should be explored. Poor involvement with the same individuals should be considered as a potential source of tension for the child.

Learning theory

Learning theory has its roots in the work of the Russian physiologist Ivan Pavlov, who was interested in the way in which certain biological events become systematically related to changes in the environment. In his famous experiments, Pavlov noticed that a hungry dog will automatically salivate when given food. Furthermore, if the dog hears a bell every time the food is presented, eventually the dog will learn to salivate when only hearing the bell and in the absence of food. This process of learning to respond to a previously neutral event is called *classical conditioning*.

Salivation is an unconditional response, that is, it is natural and reflexive; food is an *unconditioned stimulus*, that is, it is naturally associated with salivation. The bell becomes a conditioned stimulus, and the salivation upon hearing the bell in the absence of food is a *conditioned response*. A child may have a recurring nightmare at night which will eventually become a fear of darkness. These behaviourist principles were applied to the broader range of human behaviours by Watson (1930) in his psychology of behaviourism.

Skinner (1974) was a writer turned psychologist who believed that behaviour is a function of its consequences. That is, children learn to repeat behaviours that are rewarded and not to repeat behaviours that are punished. Skinner distinguished *respondent learning*: classical conditioning where the individual responds to some effect in the environment, and *operant learning*: when the individual operates or acts spontaneously upon the environment and operants are controlled by their consequences, or what follows them rather than what precedes them. Operants that are followed by reward or reinforcement are strengthened and those followed by punishment are weakened. The process of learning *which* operants or behaviours will be rewarded or punished is called *operant conditioning*.

There are two types of reinforcement. *Positive reinforcement* is the pleasant consequences of an operant behaviour, such as attention, smiling, praise. *Negative reinforcement* is when something which is unpleasant to the individual is stopped. A child may be behaving badly to receive attention, and in order to stop the behaviour, the parent, carer, teacher may speak to, distract and otherwise give attention to the child. In effect, the child's behaviour is being reinforced because he has found a successful way of getting the attention he craves. *Punishment* serves to weaken undesirable behaviour either by withdrawing pleasant things or by the enforcement of unpleasant things. Many professionals will be familiar with procedures such as 'shaping' and 'behaviour modification' which provide a way of changing behaviour by using schedules of reinforcement and punishment. Albert Bandura developed learning theory further (1977, 1986, 1992). He pointed out that there were other ways of learning apart from direct reinforcement. Children learn a whole range of behaviours through observation, such as how to care for a baby, make tea, hit others, etc. Parents and others serve as models of behaviour, and Bandura called this *observational learning* or *modelling*. Furthermore, children learn not only from reinforcements and punishments that they receive but also from those given to their models for their behaviour. In this way, children do not model *all* behaviour they observe such as stealing. Gradually, Bandura took more interest in the role that thinking or cognition plays in the mediation of social learning. There are several ways in which the child's own thinking intervenes between the observation of the behaviour and its imitation. Firstly, the child needs to *attend* to the modelled behaviour. Secondly, the child must *retain* the behaviour. Thirdly, the child must *retrieve* and reproduce the observed behaviour. In addition, the child must want to, or be *motivated* to reproduce the observed behaviour. In effect, cognitive processing of attention, memory and information processing all play a role in observational learning and modelling. Thus, Bandura redefined his theory as *social cognitive theory* (1986). Although the principles of early learning theories have found a place in clinical, educational and remedial work aimed at altering behaviour of individuals, its power in explaining human behaviour is limited. Social cognitive theory acknowledges how behaviour changes across situations depending on stimuli and reinforcement as well as the child's experience within situations. It is also a more integrative theory than the earlier theory, as it takes, to a certain extent, account of social, emotional and motivational factors which potentially influence a child's behaviour, learning and development.

Practical implications of learning theory for researchers and practitioners

1 *Behaviour can be learned, changed or modified through reinforcement and punishment*. There is need to be aware that environmental conditions can either strengthen or weaken desirable behaviour. Behaviour modification may have special applications in dealing with learning and physically disabled children and in the treatment of phobias and bad behaviour.

2 *Children learn through observing, modelling and cognitively processing the behaviour of others*. Practitioners and researchers should consider the availability and nature of role models in the child's life, including how they themselves are perceived by the child with respect to mental abilities, expectancies and motivation.

Cognitive theories

Cognition means thinking, and cognitive theories are about the ways in which children come to think about, know about and understand the world about them. The two main cognitive theorists are Piaget and Vygotsky. As with all other theories mentioned so far, they each regard the child as an active participant in constructing knowledge. They agree that both biology and environment are important, but vary on the emphasis they place on each one.

Jean Piaget (1896–1980) was the influential Swiss psychologist who was also part philosopher and part biologist. As a philosopher he was interested in questions on the acquisition of knowledge, such as what is learning? Are things always the way they appear? As a biologist he was interested in describing and recording, in a systematic fashion, the various types and stages of thought which children go through as they develop. He is credited with bridging the gap that often exists between philosophy and a science, by applying scientific methods to philosophical questions. From studies which began with his own children, he concluded that there are important qualitative differences between a child's understanding of the world and that of adults.

Piaget believed that infants are born with mental blueprints called schemas. These schemas are the primary mental organisation and structure through which the child adapts to the environment. Some of the earliest schema include the sucking and grasping reflexes, which, through adaptation, gradually become more complex schemas. This is achieved through two adapative processes: assimilation and accommodation. In assimilation, the infant imposes existing schemas upon the environment, for example when an infant spontaneously sucks anything that might be a nipple. In accommodation, the infant has to gradually reorganise the existing schema to meet the challenges of the environment, for example the many subtle changes required for adapting the sucking reflex to eating from a spoon or drinking from a cup. The child is constantly seeking a balance between the internal system and the demands of the environment, and this is known as equilibration. If there is too much incongruity between what the child is capable of and what the demands of the task are, then this will lead to excessive tension.

Piaget devised tasks and questions for children aged between 3 and 12 years and, from his observations of their performance, he formulated his taxonomy of the various qualitative changes children go through in mental processes as they mature. Subsequent research showed that it was inappropriate to be specific about age-related changes, as individual children vary enormously in their abilities. Nevertheless, it is generally agreed that the sequence of qualitative changes in cognition is sound. Piaget identified four major stages of structural reorganisation of thought processes: sensori-motor: pre-operational; concrete operational and formal operational thought.

1 *Sensori-motor Thought (0–2 years)*. This stage is characterised by beginning with reflexes which gradually become more complex as various schemas co-ordinate: for example when the child combines grasping and looking, he has a new schema for 'picking up'. Children gradually learn about object permanence, that is the continued existence of an object that goes out of sight.

2 *Pre-operational Thought (2–7 years)*. In his early work, Piaget characterised this stage by animism, realism and egocentrism, which mean, respectively, that children think inanimate objects are alive, that dreams are real physical events and that everyone sees things the same way they do. In later work, he focused on the mistakes that children make in various tasks involving logical skills. His most famous task is for testing for an understanding of conservation (of number, liquid, mass, length, area). The classic example is to present the child with two equal glasses containing the same amount of liquid, ask the child if they contain the same amount of liquid, then empty one into a taller, thinner glass and restate the question. Typically, children at this stage fail conservation tasks.

3 *Concrete Operational Thought (7–12 years)*. At this stage children are able to pass Piagetian tasks such as conservation, being better able to assess appearances and reality. They are now able to think in relative terms: that things can hurt a little or a lot, and they can grasp concepts such as 'more' and 'less'. Nevertheless, their understanding is still dependent on concrete experience of events and objects rather than abstract or hypothetical ones.

4 *Formal Operational Thought (12 years plus)*. Adolescents are regarded as being capable of formal logic and abstract thinking. They can imagine possibilities and hypothesise about relationships.

Many of Piaget's findings have been challenged or revised. It is now known that children are able to understand object permanence much earlier than Piaget believed; that children appreciate more about physical and psychological realities and are capable of passing simplified versions of Piaget's tasks when presented in a meaningful way. Inconsistency in logical operations at the concrete stage and doubt over the emergence of a new form of logic in adolescence have seriously challenged some of Piaget's conclusions. His views on schemas, adaptation and sensori-motor operations are generally accepted, as are his findings that children think in qualitatively different ways from adults, and only gradually through experience begin to perceive the world as adults do.

Lev Vygotsky (1896–1934) was a brilliant Russian psychologist whose work has only recently been rediscovered after many years of communist censorship. As an exact contemporary of Piaget, he was familiar with his early work, and produced a theory which was basically strong where Piaget's theory was weak. Vygotsky gave much greater importance to the social and cultural origins of thought and the role played by language in its structuring. Whereas Piaget believed that learning came from the inside out and the appropriate schemas and experiences needed to be in place for language to emerge, Vygotsky believed that learning came from the outside in, mainly through the use of language by older members of the community. In *Mind In Society* (1978) Vygotsky describes how cognitive functioning has its origins in the child's social interactions. A child may reach for an object arbitrarily, an adult intervenes and 'interprets' the child's action and thereby bestows meaning upon the event. In effect, then, every cognitive process appears first on the social plane, as part of joint activity and later appears on the psychological plane after it has been 'internalised' by the child. Language is the cultural tool which enables the child to internalise thought originating with others. In interacting with children, adults use speech continually to define meaning, for example saying 'one, two, three ... oops nearly fell off ... four ...' to a child as he attempts to climb stairs. Children pick up on this and can often be heard speaking aloud but directing it towards themselves, particularly when dealing with new and challenging skills. Vygotsky called this *private speech* which the child will gradually internalise, making it inner thought. This has largely been confirmed by recent studies (e.g. Berk 1994). For instance, it has been found that learning-disabled children use more private speech than normal children of the same age (Berk and Landau 1993).

An important Vygotskian concept is the zone of proximal development (ZPD). Vygotsky believed conversations between children and adults to be crucial for cognitive development. He found that a child's performance of a task when working with more able peers or with adults was a better index of their cognitive development than their performance independently. Thus a child's ZPD is defined as the difference between what a child actually achieves and what a child is capable of with some assistance. The aim of adults is to gradually remove the support they provide and pass over responsibility for the task to the child. Of course, not all parents, carers or educators are equally skilled in identifying and working within the child's ZDP. Depressed parents are less sensitive to the ZPD (Goldsmith and Rogoff 1995). It is also believed that peers are less able to work within the ZPD, usually not planning thoroughly and using less efficient problem solving strategies (Radziszewska and Rogoff 1988).

Vygotsky's views inevitably entailed a different research methodology from Piaget. He did not believe in standardised or laboratory, experimental tasks, as clearly this is at odds with his ZPD concept. In addition, because thought and its development is based in social interaction and activity, he preferred to observe children in natural settings.

More recently, theories of cognitive development have begun to consider more precisely how the cognitive function interacts with both the social and emotional functions. These theories address the child's ability to understand the thoughts and feelings of others in the social world. The methods of these theories are detailed in Chapter 7.

Practical implications of cognitive theories for researchers and practitioners

1 *Children think differently from adults and there are qualitative differences in the way children of different ages understand the world around them.* Whether you are a nurse explaining treatment or pain, a social worker assessing risks, a teacher planning a curriculum or a researcher working with children, attempts must be made to appreciate these differences and appropriate means of explaining, assessing and organising found.

2 *The child's learning, understanding and thinking is influenced by environmental conditions, social relationships and cultural conventions.* It is important to find out where the child is at in terms of experience as well as those qualitative differences which are experienced within approximate age groups. Is the child from an ethnic minority? Is there a depressed carer? How effectively are the challenges of the world brought to the child?

3 *The individual abilties of children are to be found within the ZPD rather than task performance.* Whilst there are approximate stages of abilities, all children are individuals who can, with a sensitive adult, achieve the best possible understanding and performance for that child. There are implications for people who work with children to recognise and locate the ZPD and to help others involved with the child to do so also. This is important for nurses, teachers, social workers, parents and researchers alike.

The child in context

One way of assisting our conceptualisation of the child in society is to view her as part of a social system. A system, whether biological, economic or psychological has two basic properties: *wholeness and order,* which means that all parts within are related to other parts, and *adaptive* which means an ability to incorporate other parts. An example might be the birth of a new baby into the family. This event will affect routine, require new routines and have an impact on relationships. In other words, any change in one part of the system brings about changes in other parts of the system.

Bronfenbrenner (1979, 1986, 1992) has proposed a 'social ecology' model which is defined as the progressive, mutual accommodation, throughout the life span, between a growing human organism and the changing immediate environment and the unique individual within it. Let us briefly imagine two children. One child has two parents, both working and happy in their jobs. The family lives in an affluent neighbourhood which is well serviced by excellent schools and other community provisions. The parents have a wide network of professionals, family and friends and the child is popular and clever at school, has close

6231

friends and attends a number of extra-curricular activities and out of school clubs. The family has two cars and holidays frequently. The other child has only ever had one parent, his mother. There have been male friends but no real father figure for the child. This mother is unemployed and receiving social security benefits. They struggle financially and do not have a telephone. They live in a rough neighbourhood and never go on holiday. The mother is clinically depressed, finds it difficult to make friends and manage her child's increasingly difficult behaviour. The child is unpopular at school, frequently gets into trouble and is prone to accidents and ill health. As these examples suggest, the child is part of a system or network of social and environmental relationships. There are many players (family, teachers, friends) and many settings (home, play park, school, neighbourhood). Bronfenbrenner proposed four contextual structures within which individuals and places are located: microsystems, mesosystems, exosystems and macrosystems.

The *microsystem* is the immediate setting which contains the child: the garden, the house, the play park. These are examples of physical space/ activity. Microsystems also contain people such as parents, teachers, peers and interactions with these people. The *mesosystem* is the relationship between different settings and at different times of development: links between the home and school or hospital. The *exosystem* does not directly contain the child but does have an influence and includes parental employment, social networks. The *macrosystem* refers to the broader cultural and subcultural settings within which micro, meso and exosystems are set, such as poverty, neighbourhood, ethnicity.

Salkind (1985) guides us through the model by way of the example of divorce. There are immediate concerns about the individual child and his development. We might wonder how a particular child copes with stress associated with divorce, or if it matters what the age of the child is at the time of the divorce. A specific research question might be: what qualitative differences exist in children at different developmental levels as far as perceptions and interpretation of the divorce process is concerned? At the micro level we may wish to examine the quality of the pre-divorce relationship between parents and child as a predictor of post-divorce adjustment. At the meso level we could examine the impact of divorce on the child's achievement and relationships at school. At the exo level, we may wonder about the availability of the non-custodial parent perhaps by asking: does physical distance from the non-custodial parent affect post-divorce adjustment? At the macro level there are marriage settlement issues: were discussions on child support and other concerns settled fairly and via mediation? It is also possible to consider how these various levels work in combination. In asking how post-divorce economic instability affects family relationships, specifically changes in family patterns, we are examining both macro and micro levels. Asking whether kinship and their availability assist the child in post-divorce adjustment combines issues at both macro and exo level.

Most researchers agree on the validity of a systems approach to understanding child behaviour and development. Capturing it, however, is another matter.

Practical implications of contextual theory

1 *The child is part of a 'whole' system. Getting a 'whole' picture of the child is difficult.* From the researcher's or practitioner's perspective, how possible is it to take a truly ecological approach? What are the difficulties and can they be overcome?
2 *Cultural belief systems, practices and local policies have the power to delimit and define what can and cannot be done with/for children.* Do you agree with wider contextual definitions of children, their nature and needs? If not, why not? Can anything be done about it?
3 *The child's various settings contain many people in many roles.* Practitioners and researchers need an awareness of their 'role' in the child's life and a willingness to regard the roles of others. A consequence of this is interprofessional communication and broad dissemination of research results and practice. There is a need to appreciate the methods and theories of various traditions.

Conclusion

Children are complex beings in a complex world. How, then, do we begin to research them? Their individual characteristics? Their playful interactions with peers? Their relationships with friends, siblings and caregivers? How can we capture the ways in which children are embraced, touched, punished and isolated by the society and culture in which they live? The remainder of this book is devoted to these sorts of questions.

Practical 2.1

This practical is to give you some experience of applying theory to both research and practice. Return to the three situations described at the beginning of this chapter. In groups, discuss each situation and address the following questions:

1 Which theory or theories best describe and explain the issues involved?
2 Why is a particular theory suited and why are others unsuited?
3 To what extent is the chosen theory/theories limited in dealing with each situation?

3 Theoretical frameworks

Reflect briefly on the many occasions you say 'I have a theory that . . .' followed by something like 'there is a man whose job it is to co-ordinate all your bills so that they all arrive on the same day' or 'when one baby twin dies, the surviving twin develops long-term relationship difficulties'. Whether your theories are comic, absurd or revolutionary, they are based on observation. It may be the 10th time this year that you have noticed the sickening thud of all your bills coming through the letter box at once. It may be the 4th generation in your family where the sibling of a dead twin has never had a successful long-term partnership. Some observations and theories are worth testing and some are not. If we do indeed prove that there is a Bill Co-ordinator, there is not a lot we can do about him. However, establishing a link between adult relationship difficulties and the death of a twin sibling in childhood is informative, useful and sets up an intriguing trail of research questions, answers and interventions.

The overwhelming importance of children in our lives makes them, arguably, theorised about more than anything else. When it comes to understanding and helping children, lay theories and casual observations simply will not do. A more cautious, reliable, valid and insightful approach, indeed a 'scientific' approach is needed when it comes to entering, understanding or predicting the world of children.

Approaching children scientifically

There is a pseudo debate between researchers in the physical sciences (biologists, geologists, chemists, etc.) and the social sciences (psychologists, sociologists, educationists, etc.). This debate rests upon the belief that the theories, methods and explanations one might use in investigating a digestive system, rock, fossil or chemical compound are, of necessity, different from those used when investigating human action, thought and development. Simply and correctly put, a fossil is not a human being. The matter is, however, not that simple at all when we consider how humans are also physical, biological and chemical: for instance, the way in which body chemicals control human characteristics and even how humans both adapt to and alter their physical, geographical and social environments. For researchers interested in the complex problems and the holistic nature of human subjects, the consensus is that one needs to use an eclectic or heuristic approach to the theories, methods and findings in research questions about human subjects. In the next section, we will address the traditionally distinct approaches to theory and research and go on to address their similarities, differences and potential overlaps.

The science of positivism and constructivism

The radical progress in scientific discoveries and new technologies characteristic of the industrial revolution, resulted from an approach to theory and research known as *positivism*. The positivist assumption about the nature of children is that they are accessible to the same scientific procedures one would use on a rock, fossil or chemical. Children are natural, physical beings and are subject to the same laws and principles which govern the structure of the universe. Children are determined, knowable, objective, measurable. As a research method, positivism is a process whereby the researcher seeks to establish the truth or falsity of a theoretical statement such as 'little girls who wear red shoes run faster than little girls who wear black shoes'. Such statements are also known as *hypotheses*, the truth value of which is tested through methods of observation or experiment. This method also requires systematic, controlled procedures and verification processes, the aim of which is to discover universal order, to create generalisations together with theories and laws that allow predictions across settings and individuals. The collection and analysis of numerical data is favoured, and the method is also known as *quantitative*. An often cited example of a good positivistic theory is the Law of Gravity. This theory explains falling apples, the behaviour of roller coasters and the position and movement of planets in the solar system. With very few statements about the mutual attraction of bodies, this theory explains a large number of events which can be observed or experimentally tested.

Historically, the advent of schools to prepare children for a technologically literate society, coincides with the need to better understand how their minds work and develop. Child study researchers with a positivist approach assume that law-like relationships can be drawn amongst constructs they identify, operationalize and measure. Hence, children are studied in controlled settings, variables isolated, measured and correlated with other variables, and predictions are made to populations represented by the samples being studied. For instance, a study on one pre-school may be generalised to all pre-schools in that area.

Theories of child development derive from psychology, a social science in favour of positivist methodology. Hence theories on the nature of attachment relationships between a mother and her child, based on observations of bonding instincts and behaviour in geese, can be used to explain much of, if not all of human social behaviour and development.

The trouble with doing research with human subjects – as opposed to forces, fossils and feathered animals – is that both the researcher and research participant have a conceptualisation of the research situation and what is expected to happen. The cartoon (Figure 3.1) makes the methodological point that the control of a positivist investigation is seriously undermined by the possibility of a human, subjective conceptualisation of the research situation on the part of both researcher and participant. Not only does the researcher need to contend with how the participant perceives and responds to the research situation, he is also dealing with a personality who could, unintentionally or otherwise, sabotage the entire exercise.

It is the human capacity for language, thought and action which poses a challenge for positivist methodology. Buchanan (1994) discusses how the natural processes of the physical sciences are independent of the language used to describe them, but human practices are not. For instance, a single human gesture can have several different meanings depending on the person and the context. Consider the meaning of a raised hand in the following contexts: a child in class when the teacher asks a question; a child playing in the park at football; a child waving to his mother as she leaves him behind; in a group of children who have been asked to vote on indoor or outdoor activities. Furthermore, should we wish to define the construct of 'well-being' for a child,

Figure 3.1

which definition is right – diet and exercise, normal growth and development of physical and psychological functions, or courage, wisdom and modest living? Consider how a young boy may be disturbed and angry by his father's absences yet, once a parent himself, becomes appreciative of his father's sacrifice. These examples illustrate how complex the business of interpreting and defining human behaviour is and how it is bound to the context, time and what it actually means to the people involved. Dealing with children adds further complications for positivist research. The child's capacity for language, action and self reflection is not only qualitatively different from that of adults but these capacities are also qualitatively different for different age groups of children.

There is, however, an alternative conceptualisation of the nature of children and of the theory and research methods which should be applied to them. This alternative approach is called *constructivism*. Constructivist researchers perceive the child as a subjective, contextual, self-determining and dynamic being. Children and their caretakers are social, relational beings who are engaged in joint action. As they interact they construct joint meanings within a given context. In this way, meaning is constructed symbolically in interaction with others. Children and their caretakers are inextricably part of the worlds they study. They are both the observed and the observer. Children and their relationships are dynamic across individuals, context and time. Furthermore, the meanings constructed and actions taking place in everyday situations are also located within specific cultural and historical practices and time.

Constructivists argue that, in a subjective world, where understanding and knowledge are symbolically constructed and held in convention and social unity with others, it is inappropriate to seek samples, control and isolate variables, quantify behaviour and generalise to a larger population of people. Instead the constructivist researcher makes an effort to understand how the worlds of children operate, by somehow entering those worlds, describing and analysing the contextualised social phenomena found there. The constructivist view that actions, thoughts, intentions and meanings cannot be conveyed in an analogous way with numbers, but need a more qualitative handling of data, has lead to the approach also being described as *qualitative*.

> Instead of control, constructivists want naturally occurring social behaviour, in place of isolated variables, they seek a contextualised holistic examination of participants' perspectives, instead of measuring, correlating and predicting, constructivists describe and interpret. (Hatch 1995: 122).

Table 3.1 summarises the two principal theoretical frameworks for doing research with children.

Table 3.1 *Theoretical frameworks for scientific research with children*

Positivism	Constructivism
The nature of the child is objective, knowable and determined. Child can be observed, controlled, measured and quantified. However, there is only a similarity between child and natural/ physical processes, and theories are inexact, cannot be proven, and are only probable.	The nature of the child is subjective, not objectively knowable or measurable. The child has her/his own perspective, but is also socially determined and theories are inextricable from context and culture.

Theoretical frameworks for scientific research with children

Doing research with children could be described as a systematic and scientific search for information which aims to improve our knowledge on children. This definition begs two further questions: what is meant by knowledge and what is meant by scientific? The answers to these questions rest upon which framework – quantitative and/or qualitative – the researcher has chosen to work with. In the next section we address the differing conception of knowledge and science in each framework. As a starting point, let us consider some of the sources of knowledge about children as more or less scientific, where scientific is taken to mean impartial, reliable, valid and controlled. The ways in which we come to 'know' about children include *authority*. We are told what the nature of children is by parents, so-called experts and politicians. Thus, knowing that 'children should be seen and not heard' because this is what some higher authority has told us, is not 'scientific'. Another way of knowing about children is through personal belief or conviction. So, for instance, you may be convinced that children are incapable of know-ing and expressing what their needs are despite evidence which contra-dicts it. This kind of *tenacity* is not scientific and can be tantamount to prejudice. Knowledge which passes itself off as a logical inevitability or *a priori* knowledge which 'goes without saying' is not scientific. For example, if you define intelligence as 'an innate permanent ability to adapt to the environment and solve problems' then it is a matter of logical necessity that measures of intelligence should be correlated across infancy, childhood and adulthood. A scientific test of this type of knowledge about children is likely to be disconfirmed because it fails to take into account 'other factors' which potentially affect the phenomenon in question.

There are two principal methods of scientific activity: *deduction* and *induction*. Deduction in science emphasises theories (ideas and explanations) from which we can 'deduce' likely outcomes. An example which is often given for this is that, you may never have seen an omelette fly into an electric fan but you could make an excellent prediction of the likely outcome. Induction in science emphasises data (measures, numbers, observations). In gathering data together, patterns and relationships amongst the numbers become obvious: if the numbers are 2, 4 . . . you might predict the next number as 6 or 8 or 16 but you do not have enough figures to predict which one should be next. If you obtain another figure which is 16 you can now predict the next number as 256 because each number is multiplied by itself in order to obtain the next number. It is apparent from this example, that the larger amount of numbers available, the easier it will be to reliably discern such patterns and relationships.

As a concrete example of deduction, you may start out with a theory that working mothers have poorer relationships with their children than non-working mothers. In order to test this theory, you simply challenge it by predicting the outcome in the opposite direction – that working mothers will have a better relationship with their children than non-working mothers *or* the hypothesis can be nullified to 'there will be no difference between working mothers and non-working mothers in their relationships with their children'. You then set up an experiment which will clarify the relationship between the two variables A (the number of hours worked) and B (quality of the relationship). However, in order to test this hypothesised relationship, it is necessary to define concept A and B to provide a measure of each variable. These measures can then be observed in two groups of mothers: those with little or no work (group 1) and those with a lot of work (group 2). The type of knowledge this test reveals is considered scientific because it is empirical, impartial, reliable, valid and controlled. It is also open to verification and correction, as it can be replicated, modified and improved by other researchers. If you do indeed find the answer which supports your theory, this will be a powerful scientific finding.

As a concrete example of induction, you may not have a particular theory to deduce from but prefer instead to observe, measure and examine potential patterns amongst the data produced. You may simply observe some mothers and children, noting the frequencies of things indicative of a good quality relationship, such as involvement, positive affect, etc. These patterns may, in themselves, create a theory or suggest the application of an existing one. If you do come to some conclusion, it is still scientific but not as powerful as it would be if you had made an actual prediction about what you would find.

An often cited analogy of the different ways of using deduction and induction is that of building a house. In deduction you start at the top with the roof, the overarching bit at the top and work your way down to the ground. Here you are most interested in predicting, depending on what a given roof looks like, what the house underneath should look like. In induction you start at the bottom with the ground and work your way up and stick the overarching roof on at the end in a way that explains what you happened to have built below. However, to take the analogy further, most research involving children could be described as a functional combination of both with a bit of roof or foundation to start, maybe a wall, another bit of roof and so on.

The quantitative framework for doing research with children

The quantitative research framework is based on assumptions about the objective nature of children, knowledge and research methods. Such an approach is based on the scientific activity of deduction – the procedure for testing existing theory. The notion that theory pre-exists in a law-like form is consistent with the view that the child is objective in nature and that his behaviour, understanding, knowledge or meanings are structured, determined and universal. Hence, the quantitative framework entails a methodology in which theory exists and is tested empirically to be proven or not proven. In the house construction analogy it is a top-down procedure (see Figure 3.2).

The basic methodological tool for conducting quantitative research is experimentation.

According to McCall (1994) scientific research on children entails two conceptual levels: theoretical and empirical. The theoretical level (deduction) is about general concepts, principles, laws and hypothesised relationships. The empirical level (induction) is about defining the concepts into observable, measurable variables and conducting observations that describe the hypothesised relation. McCall points out that in his simple model of a 'scientific study' (see Figure 3.3) we should be aware of the working assumptions of researchers which operate at each level. Each

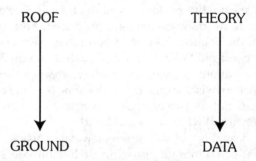

Figure 3.2 *A top-down view of theory and data*

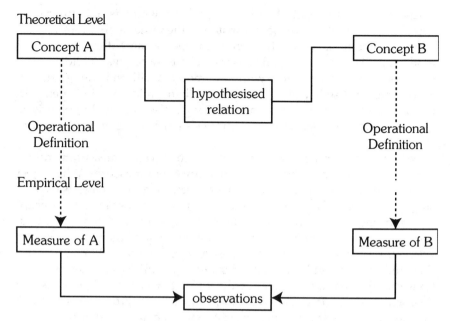

Figure 3.3 *A simplification of McCall's model for behavioural research*

Source: Adapted from McCall, R.B. (1994) Commentary, paper in *Human Development*, 37: 293–8. Copyright, 1994. Reproduced with permission

one of these working assumptions exist because researchers and their child participants are not forces or fossils and because human science is not a perfect science.

At the theoretical level, the reality of the basic concepts can be challenged. For instance, a researcher may be working on the assumption that intelligence is an innate, permanent ability to adapt to the environment and solve problems and is therefore stable across infancy, childhood and adulthood. In fact, when intelligence is tested over time, this does not appear to be the case. Whilst this could be due to a problem with measures, it could also be because the researcher is working on the wrong assumption about the stability of intelligence.

Also at the theoretical level, the hypothesised relationship between variables A and B may not be a valid one. For instance, you may hypothesise that, all other things being equal, mothers who work longer hours will be more tired and therefore spend less quality time with their children than mothers who do not work long hours. An empirical test of this hypothesis is likely to fail because, in the case of research with human participants, it's not easy to hold 'all other things equal'. Things like guilt, overcompensation and fluctuations in energy levels could easily apply in this example.

Another example could be of an hypothesis which is not sufficiently specific or comprehensive. So, for instance, the rather ambiguous and ill-defined hypothesis that 'children who spend more time with their mothers get better school grades' is much better written as 'children who spend one hour each evening with their mothers will get better grades on SATs (standardised achievement tests) than children who spend 15 minutes with their mothers each evening'. The second hypothesis is more specific about measures and implies a particular empirical relationship.

Working assumptions also penetrate at the level of measurement, influencing the quality, validity and reliability of our measures. When a test of some hypothesised relationship between A and B fails, we could simply be measuring it wrongly but it could also be because the concept we are trying to measure is much more complex than we have assumed. The example given by McCall is that infant behaviours are remarkably unreliable even across short-term observation intervals. Where, he asks, does unreliability end and lack of stability begin? Researcher assumptions can also disrupt observational control. For instance, how does one deal with findings from separate studies which compromise each other? For instance, one study reporting that children who watch more television are also more aggressive, and in another study the finding that aggressive children watch more television.

In deciding what to observe, it is impossible to do so with complete objectivity for, as Goethe noted, 'we see what we know'. Can we ever be certain that what we see is all there is? Or what we see or know is right?

Having described McCall's analysis of a quantitative framework for research in child behaviour and development, it is tempting to reject the model entirely in favour of something more qualitative. This would be foolish, however, as McCall goes on to argue:

> Suppose one defines a better football team to be one that has a better win–loss record and a poorer football team to be one that has a poorer win–loss record. Better teams beat poorer teams, everything else being equal. But if this were so obvious, no-one would play the game. The fact is that everything else is not typically equal. Poorer teams beat better teams on occasion which is why professional football fans often assert that any pro-team can beat any other pro-team 'on a given day'. The implication is that many hypotheses are not all-or-none, but are probabilistic. Even if they appear to be *a priori* in nature, our empiricism helps to define that probability, that degree of relationship, that extent of influence, recognising the portion not accounted for is due to other factors (which we conveniently call 'error' but which nevertheless consists of potentially identifiable causes). (1994: 297)

The fact is that scientific enquiry is rarely tidy, and researchers need to think more about the conceptualising of variables, specifying theoretical relation or hypothesis and ensuring reliability of measures. Even when measurement problems arise, they are still informative if only because they challenge the working assumptions of the researcher.

A qualitative framework for doing research with children

The qualitative research framework is based on assumptions about the subjective nature of children, knowledge and research methods. The qualitative approach is based on the scientific activity of induction – the procedure for generating new theories and in which theory emerges from the data. The notion that theory is created from or emerges from data is consistent with the view that the child is subjective in nature and that his understanding, knowledge and meanings are subjective, and emerges in interaction with others in a given context. Hence, the qualitative framework entails a methodology in which theory is 'grounded' in data such as observations, interviews, conversations, written reports, texts and their interpretations. In the house construction analogy, it is a bottom-up procedure (see Figure 3.4) and the basic methodological tool is interpretation.

Interpretivist scientists seek to understand the social world from the point of view of the child living in it. By way of constructs and explanations, interpretivists attempt to make sense of how children understand their experiences and how this affects the way they feel towards others. Interpretivism has roots in those branches of psychology and sociology which acknowledge the need to understand and capture subjective experiences and meanings. Humanistic psychology, for instance, begins with a view of the child as his own psychologist, creating meanings for himself out of his experiences and interactions. When a child encounters problems, the belief is that the child should be enabled to look within himself for both the problem and the solutions. Interpretative sociology encourages entering the child's world and meanings to get the

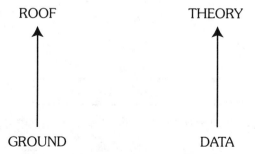

Figure 3.4 *A bottom-up view of theory and data*

child's perspective from the inside out. This is necessary because situations, meanings, problems are defined in interaction with others. The concept of labelling is a good example of how a child might be socially defined as a problem and ultimately become one.

Framework of working assumptions

How would McCall's simple model of quantitative research on children work on qualitative research at the theoretical and empirical levels, and what are the working assumptions of qualitative researchers at each level? This is depicted in Figure 3.5.

This inductive variation could also be analysed in terms of working assumptions held by qualitative researchers at each level. At the empirical level, the assumption is that it is possible to engage in methods such as observation, interviews, report or text analysis in a theoretical vacuum, with no guiding definitions, concepts or constructs. So, for instance, if your aim is to explore the quality of the relationship between a working mother and her child, it is virtually impossible to do so without some guiding perspective or sensitising concepts on what to look for, why and how.

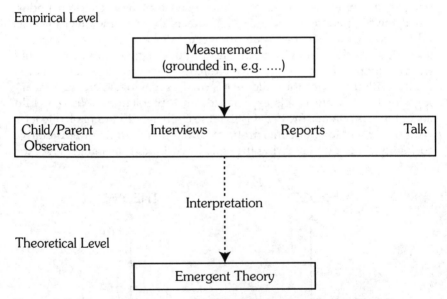

Figure 3.5 *A qualitative version of McCall's two conceptual levels of research*

Source: Adapted from McCall, R.B. (1994) Commentary, paper in *Human Development*, 37: 293–8. Copyright, 1994. Reproduced with permission

Also at the level of interpreting the research, there is the qualitative aim of discovering or entering the subjective experience and perspective of the child. Given that the researcher and participant are simultaneously both the observer and the observed, the research experience itself is mediated on several levels by the intersubjective relationship between researcher and participant. The participant has his own tacit and declared understandings, the researcher has his own perspectives and interpretations. The relationship is also mediated at a cultural level by conventional meaning systems and power relations which are interpreted within social and institutional contexts.

In essence then, the subjective nature of both researcher and participant is just as problematic for the scientific, qualitative interpretivists as it is for quantitative experimentalists.

Henwood and Pidgeon (1995) propose what they call a 'constructivist version of grounded/inductive theory' for dealing with the impossibility of atheoretical research, and they express it in a procedural framework. Qualitative researchers, they argue, *must* have a perspective from which to build their analyses and recommend a functional relationship between the data and its interpretation. In this way, the researchers' perspectives can guide the questions asked and provide a balance between possessing a grounding in the discipline and pushing it further.

At the empirical and interpretive level, in dealing with the problems of intersubjective understanding and meanings, Hatch (1995) proposes a theoretical framework based on Activity Theory. According to this theory, the goal of interpretive research is to understand the meaning that children construct in their everyday action, situated in a cultural, historical setting and in mutually interacting intentional states of the participants. This entails a method which goes beyond simply detailing what people are doing and into an exploration of the meanings and intentions which underlie these activities. The required unit of analysis includes both the individuals and the culturally defined environment which is grounded in a set of assumptions about roles, goals and means used by the participants in the activity setting.

In applying this framework to doing research with children, Graue and Walsh cited in Hatch, advise:

> . . . motivation/intention is central. Individuals are motivated to do some things and not others . . . need to pay careful attention to young children's actions and ideas. . . . To get a sense of motives, it is important to watch children's interactions closely, to listen to their explanations of actions and to be respectful of their voices. It requires basic methods of interpretive research, plus attention to the connections between the local context and the broader culture and history. (1995: 148)

In summary then, qualitative research attempts to capture the ways in which our child research participants make sense of the research events under investigation. In an important sense, then, qualitative research enables the voice of the participant to be heard. It is perhaps not surprising then that qualitative methods which specifically deal with the child's perspective have only recently begun to be addressed. As we have discussed elsewhere, the assumption has long been held that children are either unable or unentitled to have a point of view. Obviously, the younger the child, the less likely the child is to be heard in research. The dominance of the experimental method in developmental psychology has meant that the value of creating valid methods of obtaining the child's perspective in research has simply been overlooked. Attempts to address this are now proving fruitful particularly in the field of child and family social work research (Hill et al. 1996). Specific methods are detailed in Chapters 6 and 7.

Choosing an approach

As we discussed above, quantitative research demonstrates results in terms of numbers (it quantifies or measures) and usually employs statistics. For instance, measuring the effect of unfamiliar or strange situations on the heart-rate and saliva samples of 4 year old children. Qualitative research is concerned with unique situations and phenomena and would describe in detail and interpret with a view to explaining the object of study: for example, a case study of one boy's disruptive behaviour at a playgroup, with interviews of both parents and teachers about his wider social environment; or detailed, intensive long term observations of one child referred to social services. It is generally accepted in research that, in choosing either or a mixed approach, it is best to be guided by the nature of research questions, the participants, the sort of findings you require and what you intend to do with them. Figure 3.6 depicts the simple relationship between qualitative and quantitative research. The two are exclusive but have remarkable potential for overlap in practice. Multiple overlaps can be manifested in eclectic studies: for instance, an experiment on the self-esteem amongst poor readers could include some in-depth case studies of one or two children. Or a child with behavioural difficulties could be studied as a case, observed intensely over a long period of time and in a variety of social contexts, all supplemented by health and education records and interviews of parents and professionals who know the child. At the same time, the child might be assessed using questionnaires or tests on the extent of the behavioural disorder and the child's mental age, both of which are standardised and 'quantitative'. Interpretative tasks could also be included, such as measuring the child's attachment to parents through projective tests or using a technique of story completion in playing with family dolls. It may also be possible to undertake an experimental regime of 'interventions' assessing the child before and after treatment.

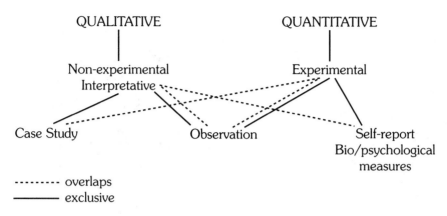

Figure 3.6 *Potential overlaps between qualitative and quantitative research*

Nevertheless, there are clear boundaries, notably in distinguishing the approaches as experimental and non-experimental. Conceptualised strictly in this way, the approaches become polarised. Qualitative becomes non-experimental research which is subjective, insider, holistic, naturalistic, valid, inductive, exploratory, ungeneralisable and discovery oriented. Quantitative becomes experimental research which is objective, outsider, particularistic, controlled, reliable, deductive, outcome oriented, generalisable and verifiable. This distinction between qualitative and quantitative approaches to research is more useful for the purposes of description and argument than it is a reality, because many psychologists and sociologists engage in a principled mixture of the two. It is a fallacy to assume, for instance, that theoreticians always behave or think like positivist or 'hard' scientists. Freud is a good example for, despite his background as a biologist and clinician whose ideas about human behaviour and development were essentially reductionist – that is, all behaviour can be explained by simple biological processes – his approach to theory, research and practice has been much criticised as 'unscientific' (e.g. Eysenck 1952). Similarly, Piaget, also by training a biologist, intent on a taxonomy of human knowledge and acquisition, and who conducted actual experiments with children, has been accused of less than vigorous scientific methods (e.g. Donaldson 1978). It is also a mistake to assume all psychologists aspire to 'hard' science. Even early in the twentieth century, Vygotsky – a contemporary of Piaget – condemned the misuse of 'positivist' approaches to child behaviour and development – such as standardised tests. These, he argued, did not address the child's individual motives, talent, potential for development or the important effects of the historical, cultural and social context upon the research situation.

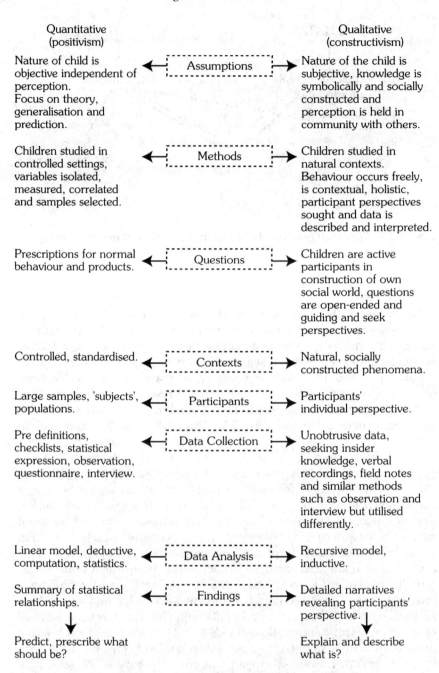

Figure 3.7 *A comparison of quantitative and qualitative frameworks for research with children*

Source: Based on Hatch, J.A. (ed.) (1995) *Qualitative Research in Early Childhood Settings.* Copyright J. Amos Hatch, Praeger Publishers, 1995. Adapted with permission

Researchers are now addressing the potential similarities or shared goals in conducting qualitative and quantitative research which is 'scientific'. There is a very good argument that any scientific research needs to have a standard of rigour which adheres to issues of reliability and validity. Both approaches can attempt to make the research in question replicable. This is a controversial issue regarding qualitative research, but a consensus is now emerging that, by documenting the decision trail in qualitative research, a process synonymous with specifying methodological details in quantitative reports is achieved (Yin 1994). In this way, it becomes more a matter of making more sense, to other researchers, of the methods used and conclusions drawn, rather than replicability. In both cases, it is essential to gather appropriate evidence so that a judgement can be made about the significance of the findings. Harding, cited in Henwood and Pidgeon,

> makes the important distinction between 'weak' and 'strong' objectivity in science: weak objectivity occurs when the inevitable layers of subjectivity are overwritten or obscured. In moving towards strong objectivity, the researcher makes public the full range of interpretative processes involved in knowledge production. Research that seeks to reveal rather than obscure the hand of the researcher and social bases for knowledge, by this account, has some claim to providing more adequate knowledge. (1995: 118)

Figure 3.7 and Practical 3.1 provide a procedural framework for choosing an approach to doing research with children.

Conclusion

In this chapter we have sought to introduce novice researchers to the different, existing frameworks or paradigms which guide research and also to the debates which surround them. We believe that it is possible, depending on the nature of your research aims, to use either the qualitative or quantitative framework in doing research with children. Furthermore, because we acknowledge the complex nature of children, we actively encourage the consideration of research designs which use both frameworks. More studies exploring qualitative methods and their application to children are particularly welcome.

Practical 3.1

Deciding to go qualitative or quantitative. This practical is to demonstrate your ability to choose a basic theoretical framework for approaching various types of research issues. Below is a list of various projects a researcher might have in mind.

Potential research projects
1 You are curious about the self-esteem of poor readers.
2 You are concerned about the body image of children receiving surgery.
3 You wonder how the birth of a new baby affects the behaviour of pre-schoolers.
4 You are interested in the effects on pre-school children who have been adopted from abroad.
5 You wonder how children feel about their parents' divorce and subsequent contact arrangements.
6 You are interested in the child-rearing practices of different British cultures.

Either alone or in groups, consider these potential projects with respect to the series of questions below which help you to decide the nature of the enquiry.

1 What is the underlying philosophical system – objective, intuitive/subjective, multiple?
2 What is the purpose of the enquiry – describing everyday reality, finding causes or explanations?
3 What is the nature of your research question/s?
4 What is the nature of the phenomenon being studied?
5 What do you think of advice from colleagues who hold opposing views on this?
6 What are your personal ideas?
7 Is there a way to use both? In everyday practice, multiple methods would be needed to explore the richness of reality.

PART II

DOING RESEARCH WITH CHILDREN – REVIEWING, DESIGNING AND CONDUCTING RESEARCH WITH CHILDREN

4 Evaluating research on children

Learning to be able to critically analyse the research of others is an important skill for the discerning professional. On the one hand, researchers themselves need to be knowledgeable about what has gone on before in their particular field so that they make informed judgements about how they should proceed with their own research. As we discussed in Chapter 1 it is important that research adds to the body of knowledge of the profession, and whilst the replication of research can be useful, it is generally desirable that research should be cumulative and build upon previous work to discover new facts or relationships. The researcher then needs the skills of critical evaluation to identify research problems which have been studied before, to explore methods and approaches which have been taken and, not least, to discover what previous researchers have found through investigation. As we discuss in Chapters 3 and 5 important decisions have to be made when undertaking research about how to design appropriate research strategies. A sound analysis of the work of others in the field will provide a sound foundation for further study by equipping the researcher with the knowledge to make informed, evidence-based judgements.

On the other hand, it is recognised that excellent practice is not only about undertaking research and pushing forwards the boundaries of knowledge, but it is also about being aware of what is going on in our own, and related, professional fields and applying knowledge to our own practices. We must, as professionals, ensure that we are up-to-date and one of the main ways of aspiring to this aim is to access and read professional journals and scholarly works. We must, however, be discerning in what we choose to apply to practice, because to apply all that we read could and probably would lead to much confusion. New and emerging theories are often reported in journals. These theories, generated through inductive processes, are largely untested, so their wholesale incorporation into practice is premature at this stage (see Chapter 3 for further discussion). However, reporting these theories is important so that debate is stimulated around a particular problem and further research in that area is triggered. It is only by accumulating evidence in a field of knowledge that a consensus view of a particular issue can be formed and tentative conclusions drawn.

It therefore becomes very important that the professional practitioner is aware of the whole, emerging debate and not just part of it. A good example of this is the contrasting opinions expressed by Browne (1989) and Barker (1990), who presented their varying opinion and research evidence in relation to identifying children at risk of abuse during the perinatal period. Clearly, a professional who had only read one side of the debate without investigating the subject more fully, might inappropriately change practice and be open to professional criticism. It is important that the reader can understand the status of a piece of research, be able to critically evaluate research and intelligently utilise the data. In the early stages of an academic debate this may mean doing nothing more than to follow the developments of the debate. Taking parts of an ongoing research debate 'off the shelf' and using bits of it without awareness or analysis of applicability is unacceptable in contemporary practice.

This chapter will follow through the process of accessing and critically evaluating the literature, whilst stressing the necessity of always placing research within a wider theoretical or conceptual frame. Two key contrasting studies, one which broadly fits within a *qualitative* framework and the other within a *quantitative* framework, will be used as exemplars of this process to give a practical focus and to act as case studies for future critical analysis.

Accessing the literature

There is an ever-increasing and wide range of sources for accessing information in a particular field. In some areas the amount of research and literature available can be daunting, making it important that you narrow down your field of enquiry. If you don't do this you may find yourself swamped with the volume of information. The process of refining your search can be difficult, and it may be necessary to undertake some general reading first so that you can identify what are referred to as *keywords*. This general reading can usually be achieved by accessing an academic library such as those found in most universities and colleges.

After you have identified your keywords, there are a range of sources which you can use to identify literature. Increased use of information technology has made this task very much easier. Computer databases, compact disk read only memory (CDROM), on-line terminals linked to external databases and the Internet have revolutionised the process, and the arduous task of sifting through cards and bibliographies in the library has become a thing of the past. The skill now is to become familiar with the technology, and most librarians will be only too happy to help.

After you have identified a range of references, judgements are required as to which are going to be appropriate for your requirements. Some information sources will provide you only with a title, whilst others will provide an abstract. Some journals are fully available on the Internet so that you have access to the whole article. The next stage is to gather your literature in a manageable, paper-based form so that you can begin the process of critical analysis. This may lead to further searching as, for example, in the case of key research articles which may reference other pieces of work which you may need to access too. If a key article appears in a particular journal and you believe the article will stimulate debate, you should access that particular journal on a regular basis so that you do not miss the developing discussion. In some professional fields there are specific and pertinent journals in which such debate will occur whilst in other professions there are literally hundreds of journals relating to a particular field. If, however, a discussion and debate article appears in a particular journal, it is normal practice for the debate to continue in the same journal.

Evaluating research

The most usual and appropriate way of analysing research is the use of the research process as a model for evaluation. However, many students, when analysing research, fall into the trap of using the research process as an inflexible model. Research should always be rigorous and scientific in its enquiry, but different approaches to research inevitably require that researchers place differing emphasis upon the various stages of the process. A *carte blanche* approach will result in confusion for the reader as they attempt to fit square pegs into round holes. The reader may make unfounded criticism of the research and the researcher. The following section gives a balanced view of how to approach the evaluation of research, by focusing on two widely available studies which adopt different research approaches so that the need for flexibility and contextualisation can be fully appreciated.

The two studies which have been analysed are:

- Deater-Deckard, K., Pinkerton, R. and Scarr, S. (1996) 'Child care quality and children's behavioral adjustment: a four-year longitudinal study.' *Journal of Child Psychology and Psychiatry*, 37 (8): 937–48; and
- Long, S. (1997) 'Being together as a family.' *Paediatric Nursing*, 9 (6): 25–8.

General considerations

The first stage of evaluation is almost an intuitive one and involves reading the whole piece of research at least once and reflecting on your first impressions. It is important to undertake this activity before you begin to engage in the fine detail of the study, when it can sometimes become difficult to interpret the whole (colloquially known as being unable to see the wood for the trees!). You become so enmeshed and engrossed that your objectivity can be compromised.

So what are you looking for at this stage? There is not, unfortunately, an easy answer, but one useful simile is to consider research as a journey. Good research can be likened to a well-planned expedition. The purpose of the journey is well defined and you know what mode of transport you must take. Your route is planned, you have an up-to-date map and you have checked the feasibility of undertaking each part of the journey in the specified time. You have done your homework and know what potential problems lie in your way. You allow extra time for these eventualities. Once you have started you do not deviate from your chosen route, and if you unexpectedly have to take a diversion or you get lost you immediately consult your map and get back on your pathway as soon as possible. You definitely don't 'follow your nose' and head in the general direction of where you believe your original path lies. When you have completed your journey you might make recommendations to other people who wish to go in a similar direction, but your recommendations only relate to the those parts of your journey which you have undertaken and which you therefore have direct experience of. You do not speculate about what you have not seen or heard.

When reading your chosen piece of research you should almost feel a sense of 'completeness' about the research. A good study should have a sense of 'flow'. The research approach should stem from the previous study in this field, the aims should be to expand the knowledge base, the methods should be justified and logical and the data should relate to the aims. You should be able to identify the sources of any conclusions and recommendations from the data. Although intuition is hardly a scientific or rigorous concept, when you become experienced at reading research you will know that when you feel uncomfortable about a piece of research, further detailed analysis will usually show you were right. If you read the piece of research by Deater-Deckard et al. (1996) you will find there is a logical flow to the study but the sense of completeness is limited in places because details of procedures relating to aspects of reliability and sampling had been previously published. The reader is given the references but would need to visit the library again to obtain the previous publication. The piece of research by Long (1997) is less complete, and the reader is left with a number of un-answered questions. For example, the study states as its purpose that understanding and the identification of the needs of parents with a new-born child requiring gastro-intestinal surgery will help them to cope. This study aimed to develop a theory relating to the needs of parents, and yet there are no concrete recommendations which could be applied to practice, and the reader is left to speculate as to what theory did eventually emerge.

After you have taken a global view of the piece of research it is time to start looking at the study in finer detail, and we have included in the following sections a step by step guide to this process using examples of real studies. Prior to doing this there are other questions which you should ask yourself before you become engrossed in detail. The first relates to the researcher or researchers: who they are; what job they do; and why they are undertaking the research. On reflection this is not such a strange thing to do. You are studying the piece of research in order to establish a base for your own study or in order to potentially change practice. Both will probably cost time and ultimately finance. Therefore you should apply a similar logic as you would if you were employing someone to take up work for you and ask if they have the right qualifica-tions for the job and what is their motivation for doing the work. This is particularly important when looking at research involving children, as we have discussed in Chapter 1. The study by Deater-Deckard et al. (1996) gives no opportunity to make an assessment of the qualifications or experience of the three authors, and only gives their places of work. The study by Long (1997), on the other hand, gives the current employ-ment details and qualification of the author, which makes it very easy to see that the researcher has experience of working with young babies undergoing surgery.

The second general point relates to the title of the work and whether it is an accurate reflection of the study itself. One of the duties of a researcher is to communicate the results of their efforts, and in order to do so the piece of research, if published, should be accessible. In an age where technology is so important and the use of databases is common-place the use of keywords to access literature has become very important, as we have already discussed. You should therefore ask yourself if the title of the work contained keywords and gave you an insight into the nature of the study. Short, snappy titles might be clever but are unim-pressive when you are searching databases and wading through hundreds of titles. The study by Deater-Deckard et al. (1996) is compre-hensive and reflects the nature of the investigation. In addition three *keywords* (Daycare, Behavioral Problems and Middle Childhood) are given at the start of this article. The study by Long (1997) would be more difficult to access. The title 'Being together as a family' does not fully reflect the nature of the study.

Introduction and the problem studied

Researchers, like most other writers, will usually set the scene of the research by formally introducing what they have studied and why. This may or may not be preceded by an *abstract* which is a brief summary of the completed research. In our two studies, Deater-Deckard et al. (1996) give a full abstract which includes reference to the background, the variables measured, the size of the sample and the findings. The study by Long (1997) gives a brief abstract which is just adequate in terms of its detail.

The introduction to the problem being studied is crucial, not only in terms of what follows but also in determining whether you feel it is worth reading the rest! Many busy people will only read the abstract and the first paragraph and discard pieces of work which don't come up to scratch, even though we all know that introductions are notoriously difficult to write and probably do not reflect with accuracy what follows. Abstracts and introductions are the gateway to the rest and should encourage the reader to feel impelled to enter to see what else is on offer. The opening paragraph of the introduction to the study by Deater-Deckard et al. (1996) places their study within a familiar context – changes in family structure and maternal employment, followed by some dramatic statistics as to the numbers of children in the USA who will be cared for by carers apart from their parent and the number of women with pre-school children who work. By introducing the study in this way the problem itself is logical in that it relates to these familiar issues. It enables the reader to relate instantly to the study rationale because we all have personal experience of, or know of, working mothers, children who are in daycare and single or reconstituted families. This is important because research should address 'real' problems which are important and of genuine concern. On an individual level, most working mothers will reflect upon how their actions will influence their children, and many will experience criticism (usually from women who do not, or cannot, work). Most working mothers will have also experienced differences in the quality of daycare provision and will probably have 'shopped around' before settling upon a particular daycare provision. On a larger scale, imagine the consequences if there were categorical evidence that daycare had long term harmful effects on an entire generation of children! The study by Long (1997) also includes an introduction which places the study within a context and introduces an element of familiarity in relation to the physical, emotional and social adjustment that is required by parents on the birth of a child. When the new-born child is ill and has to be admitted for specialist care there is an influence on parental adjustment. This study also then addresses a real problem which is of significance to the profession.

Literature review

The review of literature is a vital component of a research study, and with the exception of certain approaches to research undertaken within a qualitative framework (where the related literature is studied at a later point) it is usual to include a literature review after the introduction so that the reader can grasp what has been undertaken in this field before, thus setting the background to the study. We have referred before to the importance of research adding to the body of a profession's knowledge, and this should be demonstrated so that it becomes clear as to how *this* research will contribute to the profession by building upon what has gone before.

There are few hard and fast rules about what literature should be included, and this is largely dependent on the field of study. For example, in relation to the age of the literature used, a study which is looking at current pharmacological interventions for children who are HIV positive is likely to refer to very recent literature whereas a study looking at the long term effects of institutionalisation on adults who were in care as children is likely to use a much broader scope of literature dating back over several years. Regardless of the topic it is usual to refer to 'classic' literature and 'seminal works' even if they are dated. Each discipline has its own repertoire of such research: for example, in nursing there is Hawthorn's (1974) study *Nurse, I Want my Mummy,* in psychology there are the *Isle of Wight Studies* by Rutter et al. (1976) and so on.

All literature should, however, clearly relate to the topic under study, and the researcher should give a balanced view particularly where there is debate. The strengths and weaknesses of each piece of literature should be discussed and then compared and contrasted with other literature. The literature review should also provide a link between the problem and how it is investigated (we refer back to the notion of a good study which will 'flow'). If there is only a very limited literature review it might be that the particular journal puts constraints upon the researcher who is preparing work for publication or it might be that there is a very limited amount of relevant literature available because of a lack of previous research in the field. In the case of the latter, the researcher should tell you that this is so.

Turning now to our two studies, the literature review in the study by Deater-Deckard et al. (1996), whilst brief, is very pertinent to the field of study. The research is mostly from the USA although references are made to the situation in the United Kingdom and the Netherlands. The majority of the literature cited is less than ten years old. The literature is compared and contrasted in a restrained way which highlights the conflicting evidence in the area, which again adds weight to the rationale for the study. The strengths and weaknesses of each piece of literature are not analysed. The second study by Long (1997) used a grounded theory approach which seeks to generate data using particular methods (usually observation and interviews), analyse the data and generate a number of working hypotheses which are then compared with the existing literature (Stern 1985). The need for a formal literature review at the beginning of the study is negated so that the researcher is not tempted to 'impose' theory from other studies. Long does however review a range of litera-ture relevant to the study area at the beginning of the study, most of which is from the United Kingdom, which forms a background to the study. The literature ranges in age from 1967 (a methodological text) to 1995. As the data are analysed, further literature is cited, but the literature is described rather than analysed, making it difficult for the reader to make judgements about what is the existing research base in the field and how the data from the study compare in the fullest sense.

Research questions, aims, objectives and hypotheses

From the literature review there should logically follow clear statements about the purpose of the research, usually expressed in terms of aims, research questions, objectives or hypotheses or a combination of these depending on the type of research. In Chapter 5 we discuss the import-ance of research questions and in Chapter 3 we further discussed the use of hypotheses within a quantitative framework. Within qualitative frame-works formal hypotheses are inappropriate because they test existing theory and, as we have previously discussed, qualitative research uses inductive processes to build theory.

Aims, questions, objectives and hypotheses are pivotal to the research process which the study should address through investigation. When evaluating research the reader should seek to make judgements about the relevance of aims, questions, objectives and hypotheses and should refer back to them when evaluating later parts of the study to ensure that they have not become lost in the debate. This is all part of the complete-ness of the study. In the study by Deater-Deckard et al. (1996) the study aim is clearly stated at the end of the literature review, and the authors refer to an hypothesis drawn from a previous study. They then pose an alternative hypothesis but do not make explicit what they are seeking to test. The study by Long (1997) has a specific section to define the purpose of the study; however, as you would expect, there are no stated questions or hypotheses at the beginning, as the expectation is that these emerge from the data. Within a grounded theory approach the researcher aims to develop theory which should be ultimately testable. The study by Long goes some way towards achieving this but does not ultimately describe the theory in sufficient detail.

The sample

In our experience students undertaking research often become confused over the meanings of samples and populations, and yet understanding is important if the reader is to make sound judgements about the accuracy of data analysis, reliability and validity. Samples are drawn from, and aim to be characteristic and representative of, a population. Sampling strategies are designed to achieve that aim. If sampling is poor it can be disastrous (see also Chapter 5 for further discussion). Researchers should be absolutely clear about who or what provided them with their data and justify how they selected their sample. Within a quantitative framework the ideal is to utilise *probability* sampling where each member of a population has an equal chance of being included in the sample. In practice this is rarely possible and certainly much of the research within the educare professions utilises convenient sampling or some form of pseudo-random sample drawn from a convenient sample. Within a qualitative framework samples tend to be smaller, convenient and therefore *non-probable*, with each member of the population having an unequal chance of being selected. Qualitative researchers do, however, employ strategies for trying to ensure that their chosen sample has characteristics which are largely similar to the population from which it is drawn. One type of qualitative sampling is *purposive* or *judgemental*, where the researcher selects subjects which could not be identified through other sampling strategies, employing judgement to ensure that the sample is selected on the basis of the information required (a sort of hand picking of people who you know will have the knowledge or experiences you require).

The samples in the study by Deater-Deckard et al. (1996) were complex because of its longitudinal nature, with a four year follow-up of a third of the original children studied. In the previous assessment 120 daycare centres were selected from across three states, and children who attended the centres were then randomly selected using a stratified process; three different age groups were identified and equal numbers of girls and boys were selected from each of the age groups (or *strata*). One hundred and forty caregivers were also included in the original sample. In the four year follow-up only those children from one of the three states were included and 72 teachers. The study gives comprehensive details of the response rates for the children and the teachers and had followed-up those families who had not responded, giving reasons as to why (e.g. they had moved away). They did not follow-up the non-responsive teachers or comment on the effect of the response rate (50%). They also gave demographic details relating to the children and their mothers (e.g. age, ethnic grouping, number of siblings, household structure, maternal employment).

The study by Long (1997) gives brief details of the sample and states that 'parents were selected according to the emerging theory'. This does not give sufficient detail for the reader to know how and why the initial selection was made and what factors influenced the selection of further participants. With a grounded theory approach the usual practice is to identify an initial sample who enable the researcher to study a particular phenomenon, and further participants are selected as the researcher identifies the need to examine data further (Chenitz and Swanson 1986). Long (1997) does, however, give some detail as to the mean age of participants and whether it was a first or subsequent child for the parents. No details are given relating to other variables such as marital status, socio-economic status, attendance at parentcraft sessions, type of delivery and so on.

Ethical implications

In Chapter 8 we discuss fully the ethical implications of undertaking research involving children and what measures researchers should take to ensure that their research is *ethical*. When evaluating research it is important that the reader evaluates whether or not the researchers have followed correct ethical procedures, such as gaining permission, obtaining informed consent and so on (see Chapter 8 for a full discussion). In our two studies, Deater-Deckard et al. (1996) made no mention of the ethical implications of their study or how they addressed potential ethical issues. The study by Long (1997), on the other hand, makes clear statements about gaining ethical approval and the rights of the parents in terms of confidentiality.

As you will read in Chapter 8, following correct ethical principles is a vital stage of the research process, and researchers who do not give adequate acknowledgement to this should expect to receive criticism in relation to their omission.

Data collection

In Chapters 5, 6 and 7 we explore research techniques and ways of collecting data from children. When evaluating research it is important to identify precisely what the subjects within the sample had to do in order to give the researcher the information she wanted, what tools the researcher used to collect and/or measure the response and whether these were appropriate. Data collection tools (or instruments) include such things as interview schedules, rating scales, questionnaires, observations schedules and frequently will incorporate more than one instrument within one piece of research. Clearly when collecting data from children the choice of an instrument will be influenced by a number of factors, including the developmental stage of the child.

Returning for a moment to our completeness theme, when evaluating the research the data collection tools should appear logical and should be directed towards meeting the aims, research questions, objectives or hypothesis. In complex studies it is a useful exercise to take each part of the study and map through how each area of data collection will work. This will also highlight any assumptions on the part of the researcher and obsolete data. It is not unusual for researchers to use an array of tools to collect data which don't apparently relate to the stated purpose of the study.

The reliability and validity of the research tool are a very important part of the research process, which should be addressed by the researcher and which are rather like an internal quality assurance system (for further detail see Chapter 5). Within a quantitative framework issues of reliability and validity are addressed in a different way from that for research which is undertaken within a qualitative framework. In quantitative research the researcher is concerned that objectivity is achieved and bias is eliminated, that the study methods can be accurately replicated and that findings can be generalised across populations (Chenitz and Swanson 1986). The qualitative researcher should not ignore reliability and validity, but these are viewed differently. Replication is not generally sought, and reliability is established through verification by or with the participants.

If we look at our two studies the contrast is so evident at this point that it becomes difficult to sense that both studies could possibly fall under the umbrella of the single term 'research'. The study by Deater-Deckard et al. (1996) describes a range of data collection tools with details as to the reliability of each instrument. On the other hand the study by Long (1997) refers only to 'unstructured, in depth interviews' with no mention of reliability, validity or predictability other than that criteria were used to 'ensure the adequacy of the methodology' (p. 26).

Data analysis and results

When evaluating research it is important that the reader gains an understanding as to how data are analysed so that an accurate link can be made between the gathered data and the results. This might be as simple as a researcher describing the use of percentages or tables and graphs, or more complicated as in the use of inferential statistics. In qualitative research, data analysis may involve defining categories, employing varying levels of content analysis, coding and so on. Quantitative and qualitative frameworks may also differ in terms of the separation of actual results from discussion arising from the results. Quantitative research will usually report results in what is defined as a *value-free* way, which simply means presenting results without interpreting them in a wider context. There usually follows a distinct discussion which will provide interpretation within the context of the theoretical framework, previous work and the aims, questions or hypotheses. In qualitative research the results may be structured in a similar way, but not always. For example, as we have described previously, a grounded theory approach will describe the data generated through a particular investigation and will seek to verify emerging categories through comparison with other studies. When you evaluate data analysis and results you should attempt to make informed judgements about whether the correct techniques have been used in an appropriate way. For example, if the researcher has used a particular statistical test, is the test appropriate for the type of data analysed? If a parametric test is used are the data normally distributed, was the sample random and of sufficient size, were the measurements used at least interval and so on? (Chapters 5, 6 and 7 deal with some of these issues.) Don't worry if these questions seem daunting and alien to you. The important point here is that you should be aware that there are questions you *must* ask, even though you might need help in identifying what those questions are.

As we would anticipate, our two studies follow the two contrasting formats described above. The study by Deater-Deckard et al. (1996) has a separate results section which is followed by a separate discussion section, whereas the study by Long (1997) incorporates the two together. The first study analyses and describes the data using a range of descriptive and inferential statistics, whereas the study by Long describes categories using *verbatim* data from the interview transcripts to illustrate meaning and illustrate response and there is no separate discussion.

Conclusion, recommendations and limitations

The final aspect of the evaluation is about tying up all the loose ends and moving forwards. As with any academic piece of work the research should be concluded, and because research is about the discovery of new facts or relationships these should be defined in terms of application to practice, future research and other recommendations. These should be made within the context of any limitations of the research: for example, a study which used a convenient sample may refer to the inappropriateness of generalisation across a population and suggest that further study using a different sampling strategy be undertaken.

The conclusion is also about 'closing the loop' and emphasising the completeness of the work. We used the simile of a well-planned journey at the beginning of the chapter, so it may be useful to view the conclusion as arrival at your destination when you sit down to relax, reflect, plan what you are going to do now that you have arrived, and look forward to your next journey.

Turning for a final time to our two studies, Deater-Deckard et al. (1996) conclude their study by summarising what they had found through their investigation and by referring to how their study added to the existing body of knowledge in the field, making suggestions for further research relating to their particular findings. The study by Long (1997) has three separate sections: the implications, limitations and conclusion which collectively look at professional practice, the lack of generalisability and credibility, and recommendations for further research.

Conclusion

Evaluating the research of others is important for two reasons. First in order to be informed about the knowledge base within your own profession you must be aware of research which has been, and is being undertaken and be able to analyse that research. Second, if you wish to undertake research yourself you must be able to intelligently use previous research to guide you. The process of evaluating research is not difficult but does involve practice and a level of knowledge about the research process.

Practical 4.1: Searching for information

This practical is to enable you to practice searching thoroughly in a narrow area to help you improve your skills of accessing information. During the process of this practical keep a note of problems encountered, help received and from whom or where, solutions to problems and any other information which may be helpful in the future.

Think of an area which you might like to know more about which relates to children – if you can't think of anything look at the research hunches in Practical 3.1 (see p. 50) for an idea. Then

- Go to the library and find one general article or book relating to the topic and from there identify two *keywords*.
- Find out what databases are available.
- Ask the librarian to show you how to use one of the databases.
- Using your keywords, search the database.
- Find out which sources of information are available in the library.

If you have access to an Internet connection, using your keywords search the net to see what information you can find.

Practical 4.2: Critical evaluation of a key study

This practical aims to give you experience of critical evaluation.

- Access and look at the two studies evaluated within this chapter.
- Then select a different study, which might be one which you have identified in Practical 3.1.
- Follow through the process described in this chapter, keeping a note of any difficulties you experience.

5   Designing and doing research with children: the importance of questions

A small child who is asked the question: 'What is a Prime Minister?' may offer the correct answer, an inventive one such as 'somebody who marries people' or a comic one which has no logical relation to the question like 'a blue thing you put into the oven'. The inability to predict the answer a child will give is a fact which in addition to providing entertainment for adults, demonstrates that children's minds are special. The relationship between children and questions is special in several ways: the questions you need to ask yourself when designing research with children; questioning the assumptions behind your research questions on children; and questioning children themselves. You may wish, for example, to explore the nature of a child's relationship with his mother and to know, in particular, how the child feels when his mother has to leave him. The way in which you will go about this investigation needs to be *designed* and this entails asking yourself the following questions: What is the basic research issue? What do you want to do? Whom do you want to do it to? When do you want to do it? Are my intended methods reliable and valid?

Many basic research designs flounder because the research issue lacks a clear rationale which conveys a sense of the importance of doing the research in the first place. Thus, the following questions prove helpful: Why is this important? Who will be interested in the results? Having set up a basic design and addressed the rationale, it is wise still to challenge the theoretical and popular assumptions which may underlie it. The rationale behind this particular research issue could be based on the assumption that a secure mother–child relationship is essential for normal development. The researcher needs to consider the sources of evidence for this. Is it based on research data or clinical evidence? Is it based on popular wisdom, personal conviction or a political or professional ideal? Finally, we return to questioning children themselves. In order to determine how a child feels when his mother leaves him, the child could be asked directly 'How did you feel when your Mum left you in the hospital?' Even when put to a primary school child, the usefulness of the answer will depend upon the age of the child and also on his verbal abilities. Younger children are usually unable to cope and, in the case of pre-school children, require the researcher to enter the world with which the child is familiar – the world of stories, dolls, puppets, sand and drawing. Figure 5.1 shows some of the toys which are widely available and easily used or adapted for doing research with very young children.

Clearly, asking questions in designing and doing research with children is a skill which needs to be cultivated, and an effective training programme will deal thoroughly with the issue at all levels of research. In the following sections, we will cover these topics in more detail.

Figure 5.1   *Examples of widely available toys for doing research with children*

The question of research design

The research tutor has just handed you the Guidelines for Research. How do you feel? Your heart may flutter in excitement, anticipation and adventure at this new challenge and opportunity to systematically investigate a topic close to your heart. Or your heart may sink in panic and dread at the prospect of coming up with a topic and coping with new research skills. The best studies usually come from researchers who have a 'hunch', and those who start from this point are likely to feel positive about the ensuing challenges. The hunch may be something the researcher has observed about children when working in a school, hospital, home, or from the researcher's own experiences as a parent or child. Whatever the source of the hunch, it will be something which interests the researcher and consequently will be a source of intrigue and passion. It has been well said that the challenges of doing research are such that only researchers who 'fall in love' with their subjects to the point of total immersion will succeed! Deciding on the right questions and approaches will make the difference between an interesting study and a mundane one. Equally important is knowing why the question needs to be asked in the first place and how to do it. Therefore, before attempting to design and investigate the proposed question, researchers need to ask themselves questions like: *Why is it important to ask this question about children? Whom will the answers matter to and what can be done with them? What kind of question is it – one which can be objectively tested, a subjective enquiry or an exploratory problem?*

Why is it important to ask questions about children?

At the general level *any* question on children is important if only because of their importance in our lives. Furthermore, the climate for doing research with children has never been better, with new policies encouraging easier access to children and co-operation between individuals and agencies in order to better understand and support the developmental needs of children. Recent technological advances such as video cameras and recorders mean that we can change the sorts of questions we tackle. Subtle qualities of relationships and split second gestures are the sorts of behaviours which can be captured on camera, played and replayed and rigorously analysed on our computers which further increase our power in doing research. Figure 5.2 shows some video footage of live research the quality of which allows a detailed investigation of children's behaviour and relationships either in naturalistic or free-flow settings or in experimenter led, controlled tasks. Researchers are now well placed to ask previously inaccessible questions in greater quantities, better and quicker. Given the current climate of research conditions for researching children it is more a case of why not than why do such a

Figure 5.2   *Video footage of live research, which enables detailed behavioural analysis*

study! Other good general reasons for asking research questions on children include: how their rapid growth enables us to observe developmental changes and monitor intervention outcomes within a fairly short time span; finding out about children informs us about adults; research on children can help practitioners learn more about and improve their practice, and finally, children are often studied in order to support or disprove some theory about the nature and development of children. The relation between research, theory and practice is explored further in Chapter 2. The question may also be of personal importance to the researcher. Indeed, the *raison d'être* of the research question may be a direct result of a childhood experience of illness, abuse, adoption, emotional behavioural disorders, school experience or relationship difficulties. Finally, and perhaps most importantly, is that the research question should be important for children themselves and lead to an improvement for them and the worlds in which they live. In fact, a research question *should* be important in all the ways described.

When a research question is not a question

People wishing to do research with children come from many professional backgrounds – child health, social care and education being prominent examples. Associated academic disciplines of psychology, biology and sociology each have preferred approaches to asking research questions. In considering the nature of an attachment relationship, for example, a biologist might ask: do stress indicators in saliva increase during separations between mother and child? A developmental psychologist might ask: do insecurely attached children perform less well than securely attached children in tests of psychosocial functioning? A social worker would perhaps ask: what is the social history of this child who is insecurely attached to his adoptive parents? Clearly all of these are viable research questions but there are some important differences. The first two questions imply an objective test or experiment of some kind together with the use of specific tests and equipment. In research these sorts of questions are referred to as *hypotheses* which propose a relationship between two variables. An example could be attachment security and the child's performance on a test assessing understanding of emotion. The nature of the proposed relationships will be based on theory, in this case attachment theory, which allows predictions to be made about the relationship and to be tested in an experimental and controlled setting. Generally, a prediction is a statement that a change in one thing (the independent variable) will produce an effect in another thing (the dependant variable). Thus, a change in security of attachment is predicted to produce a change in performance of the emotion test. The aim of this type of research is to understand and explain *why* children behave as they do as opposed to merely describing it, and findings, being based on assessment of many children, are relevant to all.

Table 5.1   *Examples of research questions which are best posed as either hypotheses or as exploratory questions*

Pose as hypotheses	Pose as questions
What parenting strategies *determine* emotional and behavioural difficulties in children?	What are the feelings and thoughts of children and parents *themselves* about how they get on together?
What are the social and environmental variables that *predict* child abuse?	What are the definitions of the parents and children themselves of *experiences* of child abuse?
What is the *relationship* between family disruption and child characteristics of age, gender and temperament?	What are the *perceptions* of children from broken homes about conflict and divorce?
Emphasis is on determinants, predictions and statistical relationships. These questions seek explanations for **WHY** *children behave and develop as they do.*	*Emphasis is on description and interpretation of the participants' perspective. These questions lead to an understanding of* **WHAT** *is going on in the child's world, and the child guides the research.*

Source: Adapted from Hatch (ed.) (1995) *Qualitative Research in Early Childhood Settings.* Copyright J. Amos Hatch, Praeger Publishers, 1995. Adapted with permission

The question posed by the social worker requires a different interpretation. Here we are concerned with an individual child with a unique history. It is a matter of asking questions rather than hypotheses, and these questions are subjective and aimed at describing *what* is going on with this child. Whilst questions can be highly generalised, as in 'what is this child's social history?' they can also reflect an intention to use a particular theory: in this case, where does attachment theory inform our understanding of this child and how can we help him?

Table 5.1 illustrates the differences between research hypotheses and research questions, and Box 5.1 illustrates the evolution of a research question.

Research design: the basic questions

Once the research questions or hypotheses have been formulated and deemed important, the researcher has to come up with a basic design which addresses *what* exactly is to be done, *whom* it is to be done to and *when*.

Box 5.1   *The evolution of a research question*

Julie is on a teacher training course and wishes to work in reception classes. As an experienced classroom assistant she has noticed that very young children tend to have more behavioural disturbances than older children in reception. In addition, she has been concerned about recent government legislation which means that children can now join formal education classes as young as 4 years of age. She watches television debates and reads the national press. She is annoyed that nobody appears to be considering the long-term developmental effects of the new legislation on very young children who are, she believes, at a most critical stage in their development. She decides that this will be a good research topic and begins to formulate a number of research questions to discuss with her supervisor. Julie must first of all question her assumptions and those of established authorities. The assumption underlying her point of view is that younger children are disadvantaged in some way. Can she say that this is true of all the younger children or are some individuals doing at least as well as the older reception children? At this point all she has is an opinion based on limited personal experience and a belief based on a theory that children go through critical phases of development. She needs to question these opinions and beliefs and find 'scientific' evidence to back up her views. Julie consults a number of research journals to find out what is known about the adaptation of very young children to formal education. Julie finds that there has not yet been a systematic study of this kind, so 'scientific' evidence is unavailable. This is the rationale and importance of her study. Policy decisions are being made with the potential to damage the development of very young children whilst no investigations appear to be taking place to justify decisions. The answers to her question will have the potential to inform policy makers and practitioners who wish to minimise any potential threats to the children involved. This means that she had indeed found a topic worthy of further investigation but also that her study will be exploratory rather than adding proof to an established body of scientific research. This is the difference between asking the general question 'what are the effects, if any, of entry to reception classes on the behaviour of very young children?' and predicting a very specific outcome such as the hypothesis that 'younger children in reception class will manifest more behavioural and emotional difficulties than older children in reception class'.

Who? Given the nature of the purpose of the study and the research question or hypotheses, who should the participants be? Babies, toddlers, pre-schoolers, school aged children, adolescents, pairs of mothers and children, whole families or children from several age groups? Perhaps the study requires the participation of a particular group or a range of different child educare professionals such as social workers, child-minders, mediators, nurses, teachers, doctors, psychiatrists and service managers. Should the study include only boys or girls? Is it about fathers rather than mothers or are both equally important? Another crucial question is *how many* participants to include. If you only ask ten children to complete a questionnaire on personality and relate it to their academic performance, you would not be very confident that your conclusions are accurate. If, however, you do the same thing with thousands of children, you would be much more confident. Another requirement is to ensure that the sample is representative of the general population – in this case, to include a range of child abilities and cultures. The above example is appropriate for testing an hypothesis, the purpose of which is to make generalisations with the results and make predictions. However, large numbers are not so important when the purpose of the study is to describe what is going on in the world of a particular child or relationship.

What? What is to be done to or with the research participants? The purpose of the research may be to find out what happens when you subject them to particular treatments or conditions. If the aim is to test whether children perform better in achievement tests after a schedule of self-esteem enhancement then an *experimental* design is required. If the aim is to simply observe or measure the relation between actual self-esteem and achievement tests then a *correlational* design is needed. On the other hand, the study may focus on one particular child with reading difficulties, the aim of which is to obtain rich descriptions of the teacher's and the child's view of his reading ability, supplemented by other school, medical and social records, and an exploration of teacher strategies which do and do not work for this child. If this is the purpose of the study then a *case study* design is needed. Each of these designs and others are described in detail in Chapter 6 and the theoretical frameworks which support them in Chapter 3.

When? Do you need to assess the participants only once or more than once? A study addressing the relationship between current self-esteem and test performance need only be done once. A study comparing a child's performance on tests after intervention requires at least two assessments: before the intervention and after the intervention. Some studies which aim to say more about developmental pathways will entail continuous assessment throughout childhood: measures at 18 months, a presumed critical stage for longer term outcomes, can be related to a variety of other measures at the pre-school stage, primary school stage, adolescence and beyond. These studies which look at the same child or group of children over a long period of time are known as *longitudinal designs*. An alternative, less time consuming, approach is to study the same measures in children at different developmental stages. Thus self-esteem and achievement scores in a group of primary school

Table 5.2　*A summary of basic research designs for doing research with children*

Design	Features	Aim	Advantage/Disadvantage
Cross-sectional	Children from different age groups assessed at the same time.	To describe developmental age norms.	Quick, efficient, economic/Not about individual development.
Longitudinal	Same children assessed periodically as they grow up.	To describe developmental changes for particular groups or individual children.	Addresses continuity of development/drop outs, and participants know the test.
Correlation	Various child assessments are taken at the same time and correlated.	To examine the relation between two or more child scores and tentative explanations.	Easy to implement/cannot imply cause and other potential variables.
Experimental	An experimenter controls an independent variable or intervention.	To test hypotheses which explain children's behaviour and development.	Valuable for providing strong evidence of cause and effect in child development.

Source: Adapted from Berndt, T.J. (1997) *Child Development*, p. 60. Copyright Times Mirror Higher Education Group, Inc., 1997. Brown and Benchmark Publishers. Reproduced with permission

children can be compared with self-esteem and achievement scores in a group of adolescents. This is known as a *cross-sectional* design which is efficient but unable to map the developmental pathways of individuals.

Table 5.2 summarises basic research designs for studying children. These designs are more commonly associated with large samples of children, but most can apply to individual case studies also. An individual child can be studied longitudinally, receive experimental interventions and correlations between a variety of measures, say school achievement, social hardship, health, attachment security and self-esteem.

The question of reliability and validity

Continuing with our hypothetical examination of self-esteem, let us suppose that you wish to assess self-esteem in children who are disabled or who have been disfigured as a result of an accident. All existing measures, you think, are not specific enough about certain issues that you feel are particularly important, so you create a new version. How can you be certain that the instrument you have designed is accurate and truly assesses what you want it to do? How can you tell how good any instrument is at assessing what it is supposed to do? In order to be confident about your instruments' accuracy, you need to determine its *reliability* and *validity*.

Reliability

A reliable instrument will give a consistent measure of the behaviour or construct in question – in this case, self-esteem. If we have children complete the same questionnaire on several different occasions and the outcome varies each time from low to high self-esteem then we cannot be certain that it does indeed measure self-esteem or that self-esteem is a consistent construct in itself. Likewise an instrument supposedly assessing IQ does not tell us much about a child's intelligence if it varies dramatically between tests every Monday morning for a month. Another way of ensuring reliability is *inter-observer reliability*. This is a procedure in which two independent assessors agree on the behavioural codes being observed or the score obtained in a particular instrument. The greater the correlation or agreement between the results obtained by the two independent 'observers' the greater the reliability of the behavioural codes or instruments. If the aim is to assess, by observation, the extent of a child's solitary play, an inter-observer test would look as shown in Figure 5.3.

It can be seen, at a glance, that there is a perfect correlation or agreement in this case. However, it is acceptable to have merely good or high levels of agreement or correlation because human behaviour always entails an element of subjectivity and inconsistency (random error). In addition, where many behaviours are being assessed and/or there are many participants, it is necessary to run an appropriate statistical test (see Chapter 6). Yet another measure of reliability is the *internal consistency* of instruments such as a self-esteem questionnaire. If the instrument has 10 items assessing body image, you would expect children

Child	frequency of solitary play	
	Observer A	Observer B
1	5	5
2	2	2
3	6	6

Figure 5.3 *Example of an inter-observer test*

who score high on self-esteem generally to score high also on most of the other items. In effect, an instrument is internally consistent when all items yield similar scores. Establishing the reliability of a research tool can be a complicated and lengthy affair, so novice researchers are advised to use instruments which are already accepted as reliable by the research community.

Validity

As a researcher you need to ask yet another series of questions about your data. Once the self-esteem or behavioural scores are in you must ask 'Do my data make sense? Does this measure what it's supposed to measure?'. If you had interviewed a group of professionals on their strategies for dealing with low self-esteem in children and they spoke at length about what they do, in principle, because you know they seldom have the time to implement their strategies, then your method does not do what it is supposed to do. It does not have *face validity*. Similarly, if the group of confident children all score equally badly on your measure of self-esteem, then you need to question the face validity of your instrument and its general usefulness as an index of self-esteem. It has been argued that controlled, experimental laboratory-based research studies do not reflect the properties of the real world and real relationships in which the child lives. This type of research is said to be low in ecological validity and researchers need to be interpreting their findings from this research for real life situations. Controlled, experimental research has high internal validity, however, because confounding variables are systematically controlled for. There is quite a lot of psychological child and family research done in quasi-naturalistic research settings such as the one depicted in Figure 5.4. This shows a laboratory set-up which mimics a real domestic setting and has an observation and recording facility built-in. What do you suppose are the advantages and disadvantages of this type of research setting?

Ecological validity can be enhanced by doing more naturalistic research, in natural settings such as homes, schools, playgrounds, hospitals and neighbourhoods and using familiar people such as parents, peers and professionals in the research design. In some cases, researchers become 'participants' themselves perhaps by assuming a teacher, nurse or carer role.

Reliability and validity of methods may never be perfect. It is certainly possible for a highly reliable instrument to lack validity. Although it is more difficult to assess validity than reliability, by obtaining similar scores on a variety of instruments and measures which supposedly measure the same construct and assessing whether various scores relate in meaningful ways, it is possible to improve the validity of your research. This method is used most by researchers using a deductive model – that is, one which is theory driven and requires hypothesis

Figure 5.4 *A laboratory domestic setting with observation mirror and recording facilities built in*

testing. An equivalent method called *triangulation* is used by researchers using an inductive model – that is, one which is driven by exploratory, subjective questions and the participants' perspectives (deductive and inductive models are fully explained in Chapter 3). Triangulation enables researchers to capture, to some extent, the shifting realities of their participants. Case study triangulation entails obtaining more than one, usually three, perspectives on a given phenomenon. Research into agency thresholds in dealing with children in need could include similar interviews addressed to field workers, service managers and parents. Triangulation also occurs by using more than one researcher or a mixture of all of these.

The questioning of assumptions

It is ironic that a researcher, who has once been a child, needs to seriously consider questions such as: What is it like to be a child? How does a child think and feel? How can I find out? The feeling and thinking of childhood are lost to the adult, at least in a direct sense, for all we have are memories of varying degrees of reliability and validity. Nonetheless, until the researcher has attempted to answer these sorts of questions, there is little point in researching children at all. The best place to begin is to challenge the assumptions we typically have about children and childhood. The researcher's own view of childhood will be affected by personal experience as a child or parent; by professional training, identity and experience; by cultural views; and by current trends or fashions. Caring professions, such as nursing and social work, naturally see the child as an object of concern. A child needs to be assessed and protected, and decisions will have to be made about the future of the child. Honourable as this is, the downside is the disempowerment of the child and the oversight of the child's own perspective. The assumption has long been held that children are not able to contribute reliably towards discussions on their feelings, needs and future. This, in turn, has clearly affected the nature of the research questions which have been posed and a delay in the development of methods for speaking directly to children and eliciting their views. Certainly researchers within the academic discipline of psychology have had assumptions about children. Hill et al. (1996) describes the psychologist's view of children as 'objects of study'. This means that they too have largely ignored the child's point of view, subjective opinions and the methods which need to be used to obtain them. In effect, psychological research is done *on* children rather than *with* children. Theories and hypotheses are generated by adults, standardised tests are done on the children or controlled experiments, and the data are statistically analysed. Such psychological research has achieved a great deal in improving techniques for studying children (see Chapters 6 and 7) and should continue to do so in the future, for, as we will presently discuss, some questions need to be tackled in a controlled fashion. Professional assumptions can also influence our views of children. Teachers are likely to see them as objects of learning and development. In addition, historical or cultural trends come into play. For instance, a teacher trained in the 'child-centred' 1960s would have perceived the child as an active player in the development of knowledge, requiring only the provision of an appropriate environment and the biological readiness to learn. Compare this with the early twentieth century view of children as passive recipients of reading, writing and arithmetic. Practitioner researchers, then, should critically consider how their professional identities and assumptions of children may colour their research questions and methods. The child is always so much more than it is professionally convenient to believe.

Schaffer (1990) gives specific examples of the fashions influencing our views of children and their development. Child-rearing methods, working mothers, separation from parents, divorce, and fathers as competent carers are all child development issues which have been known to vary in emphasis over time and across cultures. Schaffer also warns of the danger of forming beliefs about children based on the wisdom of established authorities. It often is the case that such wisdom is derived from a mixture of personal opinion, guesswork, folklore, work with clinical cases and experiences of rearing their own children. Indeed, this is true, to some extent, of some of the most influential developmental theorists, including Darwin, Freud and Piaget!

Questioning adults about children and childhood

In some types of research it may be necessary to question an adult on the child's behalf. This is likely to be the case when the child is too young or unable to speak. It could also be that it has been deemed unethical to raise particular types of questions with children directly or that the researcher has a particular interest in the parent's or carer's relationship with the child or the perspective of the child. Another approach is to assess the parent's own experiences of childhood and perhaps relate them to how they perceive and relate to their own children. All of these approaches are important and relevant for anyone doing research with children. Regardless of the focus of the main research question, a questionnaire or an interview with an adult or parent who knows the child well can add a new dimension to the research. The techniques for interviewing parents and adults who care for or work with children are discussed in detail in Chapter 7.

Questioning children themselves

The novice researcher about to question children for the first time will have to deal with a number of myths which surround the whole process. Typically these include assumptions about the child's capabilities. Notions that young children cannot be asked direct questions or chatted to are common, as are beliefs that they should not be seen alone or for any length of time. Nonetheless, in the context of the child's age, there are important issues which do need to be taken into account. Very young children or pre-schoolers do have limited communicative abilities relative to school-aged children. On the other hand, they are also surprisingly competent in ways not usually appreciated by researchers. The issues primarily concern the cognitive abilities of the children, the validity of their statements and researchers' interpretations of their statements.

Whilst reliability is important for specific measures, it is mainly validity that matters when verbally engaging with children. The accuracy of children's responses largely depends on their developmental capacities, including their ability to understand the questions being posed and the reason for the interview. Every effort should be made by the researcher to understand the child's developmental and individual abilities and to explain why the child is there and what will happen. Researchers should present themselves in a friendly and reassuring manner and the child should be allowed time to become familiar with a strange environment or new pieces of equipment or toys that are part of the research. Let us consider some kinds of questions a researcher might want to put to a child.

Who? What? Where? Very young children are able to identify people, objects and places either verbally or by pointing to them. They can distinguish self from others. Very young children, however, are prone to errors of classification: all male adults could be labelled 'daddy'.

Why? When? How? Even though 2 year olds can make simple inferences about cause and effect and understand the permanence of objects, it is not until reaching school age that children are consistently able to respond to questions requiring explanations such as 'why?', 'when?' or 'how?'.

The past, present and future Pre-schoolers are able to talk about present and past experience, but their concept of time is not fully developed. Order of recall and use of past tense is not always easy for them. Around 4 years of age, they are using past and future tenses but their notions of time are still associated with routines such as meals or television programmes. Their concept of time improves gradually once at school and they become able to deal with clocks and calendars.

Questions relying on memory A related issue is the memory capacity of children. Like adults, a child's memory can be affected by other factors such as the circumstances around the event in question and associated emotional arousal. Children will not be comparable to adults until the end of the primary school years. Consequently, young children often need support in remembering, and this can be improved by using familiar toys and allowing the child to play or enact past events with the help of toys. This enables a researcher to clarify who or what the children are talking about.

Sensitive questions The child's ability to distinguish fact from fantasy is important in questioning a child about a traumatic event, as is the researcher's ability to interpret what the child says and does. Even quite young children do not create a false picture. Three year olds are able to tell the difference between pretend play with materials and its real nature, and 4 year olds understand the difference between truth and lies and that telling lies is wrong.

Interpretation of child's response

Children's self reports are vulnerable to suggestibility and denial and are therefore influenced by the status of the interviewer. It is generally believed, however, that events which are important to the child are fairly resistant to such distortion. In disclosing painful experiences, children may experience anxiety which either prevents the child from speaking about it, deny it or change their minds. Fears of losing loved ones, punishment of self and others and rejection are common.

Children's drawings

Children's drawings are believed to reveal the child's inner mind. The clues are believed to lie in the child's alterations of line quality, disguising shapes and using unusual signs or symbols. One of the easiest and most common drawing tasks for children is the 'draw a person, draw a house, draw a tree' task. This is depicted in Figure 5.5 together with a case outline of the two children who drew the respective pictures. Child A's drawings are depicted on the left of the photograph above. He is seven years old and has been physically abused. His parents have a history of mental ill-health. He is rejected and bullied at school. Child B's drawings are depicted on the right of the photograph above. He is a happy, normal seven year old. One is immediately struck by the impoverished work of child A in terms of size, detail and imagination. There are a number of other indicators in drawings. Anxiety is represented through intensity of line pressure, excessive shading, smallness of the figure and rigidity of the drawing process. Abused children may include sexualised body parts or shaded over body parts and sad or expressionless figures. Heavily scratched areas and repeatedly overworked lines across the body or torn hands may indicate physical abuse. Of course, drawings are particularly susceptible to false interpretations of the questioner, and it is crucial for these drawings to be correlated with a variety of other sources of information and to operate in an open, exploratory manner with children and their drawings. See Box 5.2 for guidelines on questioning children and interpreting their answers.

Figure 5.5   *A comparison between a neglected child and a normal child on the 'draw a house/tree/man' task*

Box 5.2   *Improving the validity of questioning and interpretation of answers*

Improving validity: questioning

- Break complete events or issues into simple, manageable units for pre-schoolers who are unable to keep two concepts in mind at once. Use simple yes/no questions followed by more open-ended ones. Use familiar toys to clarify identities and demonstrate events.
- School-aged children can be expected to gradually understand and use more complex sentences.
- Children occasionally tell stories which parents know did not happen. In taking their capability to distinguish fact and fantasy and the possibility of denial into account, be prepared to accept an unclear conclusion
- Ask the child if particular fears are affecting what they say.
- Take individual differences into acount. Some children may be learning disabled or may prefer to reveal information slowly over longer periods of time.

Improving validity: interpretation

Children's reports are more likely to be valid:

- where the child uses age-related language;
- where the account is relatively detailed for the child's age;
- where the child displays appropriate emotional behaviour;
- where younger children express emotional feelings behaviourally rather than in a detailed verbal account;
- where a child's report is consistent over time;
- where hesitancy is evident during traumatic disclosures.

Source: Adapted from Reder, P. and Lucey, C. (1995) *Assessment of Parenting.* Copyright Routledge, 1995. Reproduced with permission

The child's perspective

Listening to the voices and views of children themselves is one of the most neglected aspects of child developmental research. It has been too long assumed that children have little to add to research that is valid and also that the whole business of the child expressing a point of view or desires is too distressing for the child and therefore is ethically unsound. Nonetheless, the 1989 Children Act has set up a legal requirement to consult the wishes and feelings of children when assessing their physical, emotional and educational needs. The Act has not only had a direct impact on the decision makers, agencies and educarers who deal with children on a daily basis, but also kindled the interest of researchers, especially practitioner researchers, in designing and improving the reliability and validity of techniques of obtaining the child's perspective in the light of what we do know about the child's age and understanding. Methodological considerations in obtaining the child's perspective are dealt with in detail in Chapters 6 and 7.

Practical 5.1

The 'I've got a hunch' exercise. This practical is to further demonstrate that you already possess a basic aptitude for posing research questions and hypotheses and designing approaches. You may do the practical alone or your tutor will divide you into relevant groups/pairs sharing an interest (e.g. education, health/nursing, social work). In these groups, discuss the following series of research 'hunches' in terms of:

- the type of study (qualitative, exploratory, experimental, etc.);
- defining the problem to be researched;
- the importance of the question and practical applications of the answers;
- possible research questions or hypotheses;
- who the subjects should be and their characteristics;
- possible assessments, materials and equipment;
- problems anticipated in doing the research.

Research hunches
1 You are curious about the self-esteem of poor readers.
2 You are concerned about the body image of children receiving surgery.
3 You wonder how the birth of a new baby affects the behaviour of pre-schoolers.
4 You are interested in the effects on pre-school children who have been adopted from abroad.
5 You wonder how children feel about their parents' divorce and subsequent contact arrangements.
6 You are interested in the child-rearing practices of different British cultures.

---

6 Classic methods for doing research with children

Below is an extract from Piaget's baby biography of his daughter. The numbers represent years, months and days:

> At 0:4(23) without any previous practice, I showed L my hand which I was slowly opening and closing. She seemed to be imitating me. All the time my suggestion lasted, she kept up a similar movement and either stopped or did something else as soon as I stopped. There was some reaction when I repeated the experiment at 0:4(26). But was this response of L merely due to an attempt at prehension? To test this, I showed her some other object. She again opened and closed her hand, but only twice, then immediately tried to seize the object and suck it. I resumed the experiment with my hand, and she clearly imitated it, her gesture being quite different from the one she made on seeing the toy. (1945/62:23)

In this example, Piaget is clearly conducting an informal experiment. There appear to be at least two explanations for the observed behaviour, and Piaget tests his hypotheses by some simple manipulations and, perhaps not surprisingly, finds support for his preferred explanation. This one, small vignette shows Piaget engaging in a variety of methods which have become better defined in recent years. Methods of observing and recording data, of conducting experiments, of assessing the motor and psychological functions of children, have become so rigorous that baby biographies like Piaget's are no longer regarded as reliable and valid. In this chapter, we describe and discuss classic research methods of observation, correlation, experiment, survey, case study and ethnography.

Observation

In a sense, all research involves observation. If the purpose of research is to improve our understanding of an individual, a relationship, a particular social group or culture, then that knowledge begins with observation. Observation means watching children individually, in relationships, in contexts and asking: what do they see, what do they feel, what do they think, what do they do? This is a procedure which empowers the child whose silent 'voice' is heard by the researcher, but also empowers the researcher herself. The process of observation takes the researcher on a personal voyage around her own perceptions, feelings, thoughts and actions which can be both disturbing and liberating. Figure 6.1 illustrates how a competent observer is able to integrate and reflect upon several perspectives at one time, in a given research situation. It also shows how other aspects of learning can follow from observing (Trowell and Miles 1996). As a basic technique then, observation underpins a variety of approaches to research. There is also a variety of observational techniques to consider. *Naturalistic observation* is a technique used by ethnologists who study behaviour in its natural settings; *controlled observation*

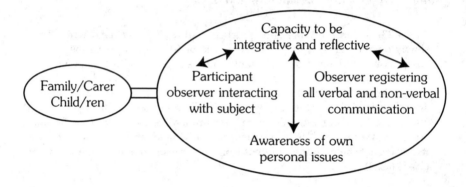

Ways of considering observation material

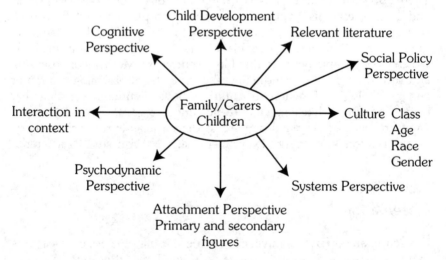

Figure 6.1   *Developments in the observer's mind during observation*

Source: Trowell, J. and Miles, G. (1996) 'On the outside looking in.' *Journal of Social Work Practice.* Carfax Publishing, Abingdon. Reprinted with permission

still involves spontaneous behaviour but in a situation which to some extent has been manipulated by the observer – an example is Ainsworth's strange situation (see below); using archival data or social statistics could be described as *indirect observation* or *content analysis* – that is, frequency counts of certain phrases or words in a communication, is a form of observation. When the observer becomes part of the group he or she is studying, it is known as *participant observation*; this includes a social worker working in a social services agency to discover how many child referrals to such agencies are handled or an undergraduate working in a school to discover how teachers define quality of curriculum. In *non-participant* observation the observer only watches; this could be a psychologist behind a two-way mirror watching the free play interactions between a mother and her infant and coding behaviours. Finally, when an observer participates, but does not inform other participants of his role, it is called *undisclosed observation*.

Observational techniques are particularly helpful for doing research with young children who may be unable to communicate any other way. There are other sound reasons why it is desirable to research children in their natural environments, such as the home, school or neighbourhood rather than subject them to experimental manipulations. For one thing children are particularly reactive to strange people and strange situations. Another reason is their vulnerable position regarding informed consent (see Chapter 8). There are various ways of observing children, and these vary according to the age of the child, their conceptual abilities, their relationship with the observer and, of course, the purpose of the research.

The most popular child observation techniques are the Tavistock Model and The Ethological Target Child Method. Both are naturalistic and qualitative, but the Ethological Model can also be quantitative. Each model also uses participant and non-participant observation in different ways.

The Tavistock model

The Tavistock Model of Infant Observation was pioneered by Esther Bick in 1948 as a training programme, the purpose of which was to teach trainee psychotherapists to observe well. As such, it serves as an excellent model for anyone who wishes to work with or do research with children, for it simply teaches one to observe. Although the programme was aimed originally at psychoanalysts, its power to develop professional observation skills has been noted and widely used by other professional groups such as social workers, clinical psychologists and educational psychologists. Nevertheless, practitioners and researchers who embark on the Tavistock method of observation necessarily submit themselves to forms of psychoanalytic induction.

Trainee observers are closely monitored in 'state of mind' seminars during which the leader acts as a kind of analyst and fields the group discussion of fellow observers around the experiences each group

---

Box 6.1   *The Tavistock model of observation*

How it's done

1 Naturalistic observation of infants at home.
2 Observer ideally meets parents before baby is born.
3 Baby is visited/observed for one hour each week until the baby's second birthday and at the same time on the same day each week.
4 No note taking, but recall all events that took place during the visit afterwards.
5 Emphasise what is seen and felt instead of looking for what you think should be there.
6 Regular seminars with a seminar leader and fellow observers to discuss observations, feelings and interpretations.

Why it's done

1 Allows observer to experience emotion of infancy when discovering our place in the world.
2 Sensitises observers to emotional atmosphere in which the baby lives and grows. Links between feeling states of mother and child, between actual supports to mother and her capacity to support physical, emotional and cognitive needs of the child.
3 Learn about the impact of sexual identity, family position, class, race, culture, effects of child-rearing patterns on child development, unemployment, divorce, death, illness – the infinite variety of life situations.
4 A searchlight on the origins of emotional disturbance, allowing exploration of links between emotion and cognition and insight into the nature–nurture debate. Patterns emerge.
5 Hypotheses can be made and tested throughout observation. Follow-up and methodology can be described, developed and adapted to follow infants into adulthood. Received wisdom can be challenged.
6 Makes theory reading dynamic, interactive, and stimulates observer intellectually and emotionally, improving critical and reflective powers.
7 Reaches people previously considered unsuitable for psychoanalytic psychotherapy.

Source: Adapted from Reid, S. (ed.) (1997) *Developments in Infant Observation: The Tavistock Model.* Copyright Routledge, 1997. Reproduced with permission

member has of their observation placement. Trainees are reflecting and integrating not only the experiences of the infant they see, but on their own experience of the observational encounter. Some key psychoanalytic concepts such as *containment* are relevant to both carer and observer. Containment is about attention. The ability to suspend one's own needs and wishes in favour of those of another and which may result in feelings of gratitude and loving, caring acts in return.

Tavistock observers get to 'know' their infant and carers intimately. The intensity of this type of observation is exhausting and demanding but also rewarding. Box 6.1 summarises the basic Tavistock Model of infant observation and the reasons why it should be done.

It is worth exploring the kind of *participant observation* required for the Tavistock model. They favour an approach in which the observer

Figure 6.2

becomes a friend with her subjects and interacts with them in the most trusted way possible. As the cartoon (Figure 6.2) suggests, it hardly makes sense to think about participant observation with infants. Fine and Sandstrom (1988) point out that one can observe and interact with them, but can one really participate in a meaningful group life? In the Tavistock Model, then, observers are participating in the family life, or the carer–child relationship.

The analysis of this type of observation is open and interactive. Observers recall what was seen and felt by both their participants and themselves. Vignettes of recalled events and feelings can be put into a narrative account and presented to other seminar group members for discussion. As part of a course assessment, students are often required to keep a reflective diary of activities, events, thoughts and feelings.

The ethological target child method

Sylva et al. (1980) have adapted the 'follow individual animals' method of ethology into a 'follow individual children' method for use in the natural pre-school habitat. The 'target child' method entails following a particular child around, taking detailed field notes of their behaviour for analysis later on. As a detailed, qualitative study of individual children as they interact with their physical and social environments, this method is favoured by education practitioners who wish to improve the learning environment for children, but it can readily be adapted by other educare practitioners and researchers. They may wish to monitor specific situations such as the 'new' child, a 'problematic' baby, or to improve the provision of materials, equipment and activities in the learning environment. Other examples include: examining the nature of interactions between teacher and pupils and the amount of time children spend on and off tasks. Because the flow of behaviour is recorded over a time period it is possible to obtain frequencies of activities/behaviours per minute, and these data are useful for making comparisons between larger groups of children, say bullies and victims or boys and girls. It is, then, essentially a qualitative method which can be participant or non-participant. However, quantitative data can be obtained and can allow comparisons between existing groups created by, for instance, age and gender.

Observers need to select a target child, perhaps the 'new' child or a 'bully', or whenever there is an obvious reason to get a detailed observation of that child. Where the child himself is not the focus then choose a child randomly. It may be helpful to dictate observations into a small dictaphone for transcribing and timing later.

Observations are recorded on a proforma, or observation sheet in the form of short-hand codes and long-hand details providing an account of what the child is doing, saying and with whom. Double lines across the page indicate a change of activity then. Figure 6.3 shows a basic coding sheet and what it looks like coded. The information entered will be quicker to enter, read and understand if codes are used. Box 6.2 shows a summary of codes used in this method.

Holmes and McMahon (in Sylva et al. 1980) recommend using target child observation as a part of student group discussions which help to understand the method and reason for it. Groups should discuss issues such as:

1 Really seeing what the child is *doing*.
2 What is the child *talking* about?
3 With *whom* does he play?
4 Did the child spend much time watching?
5 Did the child do the same thing or several different things?
6 What made him start/stop?
7 How satisfying was the activity to the child? What is your evidence?
8 Has your observation given you fresh insights about the child or pre-school provision?

This observational method is flexible and can be adapted to suit particular research interests and questions. You could devise a coding scheme

Child's Initials: *TC* Sex: boy Age: 4.2 Date: 6/6 Time: 10.10am			
Activity Record	Language Record	Task	Social
TC joins a group of 3 children at the art table and starts drawing.	*TC sings to self*	*ART*	*SGp*
Teacher joins group, TC asks for help and teacher responds and then demonstrates.	*TC → A show me how to do a spider A → I'm afraid of spiders*	*ART*	*(SG)*
Child gets bored, moves towards a group of 6 children doing LEGO and starts to build own model beside a helper.		*SCC*	*(LGp)*

Figure 6.3 *The target child method – example of an observation proforma and recorded observation using codes*

Source: Adapted from Sylva, K., Roy, C. and Painter, M. (1980) *Childwatching at Playgroup and Nursery School: Oxford Pre-school Project Grant.* Copyright Sylva, Roy and Painter, Grant McIntyre, 1980. Reproduced with permission

which taps more precisely the forms of behaviour in which you are interested. However, if you devise your own coding scheme or use an existing one, issues of reliability and validity need to be addressed. This is explored in Practical 6.2.

Other variations on this type of observation include: the use of checklists; time sampling and event sampling, each of which is more economic than free-flow behaviour sampling both in terms of time and in addressing particular research questions.

Box 6.2   *Target child observation codes*

Participation & language code

(what is said by whom to whom)

TC	Target child
C	Other child
A	Any adult
→	Speaks to

(e.g. TC → C I'm dad, you're mum)

Social code

(whom the child is with)

SOL	Solitary
PAIR	Pair
SG	Small group
LG	Large group (6+)
p	parallel
O	circle around child code: with/near adult

Task codes

LMM = large muscle movement
LSC = large scale construction
SCC = small scale construction
ART = art
MAN = manipulation
ADM = adult directed art/ manipulation
SM = structured materials
3Rs = 3 Rs activities
EX = examination
PS = problem solving
PRE = pretend
SVT = small version toys
IG = informal games

GWR = games with rules
MUS = music
PALGA = passive adult-led group activity
SINP = social interaction, non-play
DB = distress behaviour
SA = standing around/aimless
CR = cruise, purposeful looking
PM = purposeful movement
W = wait
WA = watch
DA = domestic activity

Source: Adapted from Sylva, K., Roy, C. and Painter, M. (1980) *Childwatching at Playgroup and Nursery School: Oxford Pre-school Project Grant.* Copyright Sylva, Roy and Painter, Grant McIntyre, 1980. Reproduced with permission

Figure 6.4 shows what observation sheets would look like for each of these procedures, and Box 6.3 shows one of the many ways in which observational techniques can be adapted for research.

Observing a child in the natural environment will give research a 'real world' edge to it. The technique is especially favourable for young children, sick children and children with special learning or physical needs. These things instantly give the work high external/ecological validity. This can be further enhanced by minimising the degree of intrusion by way of non-participant and 'friendly' participant observation. Data collection needs to be unintrusive and slick and can be aided in some situations by the use of concealed or discreet video cameras, portable voice-activated tape recorders or dictaphones, well-designed, economic recording sheets and stopwatches. A well-designed observational study will also enable the researcher to record these real life events as they occur. This direct experience facilitates the researchers' ability to understand complex individuals and situations and to build upon

Time	On task involved	On task uninvolved	Off task quiet	Off task disruptive
10.00	✔			
10.01	✔			
10.02	✔			
10.03		✔		
10.04		✔		
10.05				✔

(a)

Sheridan's norms of child development (4.5 years)	Yes	No	Comments
1. Affectionate, confiding	✔		holds friend's hand and whispers
2. Likes to help domestic chores	✔		readily agrees to help wash up and took interest in how clean cups were
3. Tries to keep environment tidy		✔	messed toys and ran away when asked to tidy up
4. Symbolic play	✔		imaginary friends to tea
5. Joins in symbolic play	✔		playing weddings with friends each with a role
6. Shares toys	✔		

(b)

Time	Activity	Language	Social
9.00	TC joins friend at climbing frame	TC → C I can go higher than you C → TC can't	PAIR
9.01	TC pushes C off frame	TC (laughs)	PAIR
9.02	C pushes TC off frame	C → TC I was here first, but you can stay	PAIR

(c)

Time Onset	Time Offset	Event (coded) (note, where possible, events preceding + following aggressive events)	Language	Social
9.15	9.18	(PA) + (HA) TC pulls hair of C viciously and she cries	TC → C I hate you	PAIR
9.19	9.20	(VA) TC sneers at C	TC → C You're an ugly sissy	PAIR
9.21	9.22	(PA) TC pushes C on floor		PAIR

(d)

Figure 6.4   *Special forms of observation: (a) checklist precoded for time and onset/offset of tasks and level of involvement; (b) checklist using norms of social development scale, for a 4.5 year old; (c) time sampling of target child; (d) event, sampling of target child. Codes: PA, physical aggression; HA, hostile aggression; VA, verbal aggression*

theories. The method, however, does not adapt well from single individuals or simple settings to large groups or complex settings and thus limits the possibility of making comparisons and contrasts. This fact, together with the lack of control over 'other' variables, mean that explanations of what is observed are necessarily interpretative and correlational rather than causal. However, because observation does not have the predictive power of experimental designs (see Chapter 3), it is important not to regard it in any way as inferior or easier to do. As has been already noted, the procedure is not only personally and emotionally demanding on the researcher, it is also regarded by most as prior to and superior to the experimental method. Box 6.3 illustrates an observational procedure using a version of a rating scale.

Box 6.3   *An observational instrument from a study on the comparison of anxiety-reducing potential of two techniques of bathing*

Child identification code:
Date:

Behavioural cues:
while observing patient/child indicate the category of behaviour as follows.

Body activation (circle one)

severe anxiety – continual non-purposeful activity or inactivity
mild anxiety – some motions not purposeful, activity increase on mentioning pain/operation
no anxiety – gestures purposeful and appropriate

Facial expressions (circle one)

severe anxiety – frowning, down turned mouth continually
mild anxiety – occasional facial expression of anxiety
no anxiety – content and pleasant facial expression

Vocalisations (circle one)

severe anxiety – sighing, inappropriate laughter, 'I don't know', desperate, panicky, terrified
mild anxiety – angry, depressed, uncomfortable, nervous, frightened
no anxiety – use of non-anxiety words: happy, optimistic, secure

Conversation (circle one)

severe anxiety – expresses numerous concerns, worries, complaints, inability to focus on interview
mild anxiety – occasional expression of worries, complaints
no anxiety – no expression of dissatisfaction and/or expressions of contentment

Source: Adapted from Barsevick and Llewellyn (1982), 'A comparison of the anxiety-reducing potential of two bathing techniques.' *Nursing Research*, 31. Reproduced with permission

Correlation

In everyday language when we say that two things 'correlate' we mean that they 'go together' and are related in a systematic way. If you have been following crime reports in the newspapers in which young children are involved whilst also taking note of the truancy rate at the school in which you work, you may notice a correlation between these two obser-vations. Perhaps as the truancy rate rises, so also do the number of reported crimes committed locally by children. This would be a positive correlation. On the other hand, you may observe that as the truancy rate increases, the crime rate decreases. This would be a negative correlation. Of course it could easily be that there is no correlation in that sometimes truancy and crime go together and sometimes they do not. The relation-ship can be depicted as in Figure 6.5.

In this way the direct linear relationship between the two observations can be seen. If there were a perfect correlation between them it would be possible to draw a perfect straight line across the graph.

The symbol for correlation is 'r'. It is measured on a scale of 1, with 1 being a perfect positive correlation, 0 no correlation and –1 a perfect negative correlation. Figure 6.6 depicts various degrees of correlation and their 'r' coefficient or score.

Strictly speaking, correlation is not a *method* but a technique of data analysis. Data analysis is beyond the scope of this book, but correlation is worth mentioning here because of its usefulness in analys-ing observational data and in establishing the reliability or validity of observational schemes and codes. As a data analysis technique, corre-lation tests whether such a systematic relationship exists between

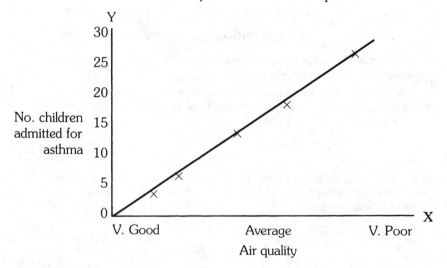

Figure 6.5   *Hypothetical correlation between air quality and emergency hospital admissions of child asthma sufferers*

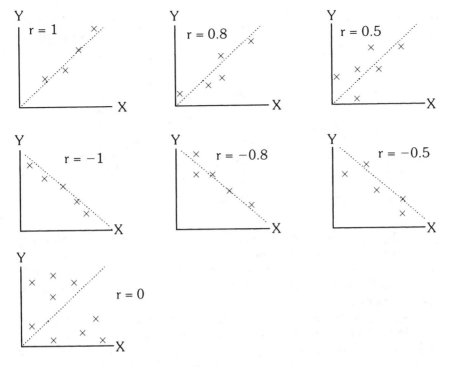

Figure 6.6 *Hypothetical correlations*

two or more variables. An explanation for the existence of any relationships found cannot be proved by such a test, but can only be inferred and discussed as a possibility. Therefore, it is inappropriate to talk about independent and dependent variables (see Chapter 3). We can, however, speak of 'co-variables'. Because correlation lacks control and manipulation of variables, it shares the same sources of internal invalidity as naturalistic observation. This makes it a frequently used tool in observational studies for suggesting possible relationships and directing further enquiry.

What then can a correlation score or coefficient tell us and what can it not tell us? Firstly, because there is likely to be a number of factors co-varying we cannot say that X causes Y or Y causes X. A positive correlation between truancy rates and child crime in a particular town cannot be expressed as 'truancy *causes* crime'.

A positive correlation between children watching violent television and aggressive behaviour cannot be expressed as 'watching violent television *causes* children to behave aggressively', because it can also be said that 'aggressive children prefer violent television'.

The X-Y relationship may also be related in a systematic way to a third, unobserved variable: a positive correlation between IQ and head size in primary school children is likely to be *confounded* by age.

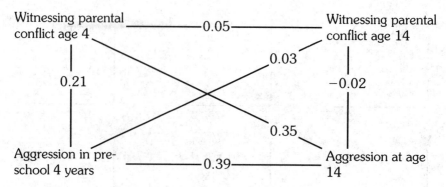

Figure 6.7 *Hypothetical cross-lagged correlation data*

Finally variables can be systematically related, such as the relationship between memory and age, but in a curvilinear way. A correlation test using the Pearson R, which assumes a linear relationship, would imply, falsely in this case, that there is no systematic relationship between age and memory.

Some correlational studies attempt to improve internal validity by looking at patterns of correlation in longitudinal designs. The underlying assumption is that if one variable causes another, the first (say witnessing parental conflict) should be more strongly related to the second (say aggression) later in time than when the aggression was measured in the first place. In a sense, it is saying that causes should take some time to produce their effects. However, as correlation is only a method of agreement, it can only enhance the possibility of an explanation. Figure 6.7 shows an imaginary longitudinal (cross-lagged panel) correlation study. The important data are on the diagonals.

Experimental method

What is an experiment? Here is a very nice example. Mums love babies and babies love mums. How does their attachment develop? It is obvious from observation that baby depends on mum for care, especially *food*. Mum also handles and cuddles baby a lot at feeding time. According to Freud's theory, babies have innate oral drives which mums satisfy. This leads to the view that it is the feeding function which causes 'love'. Harlow (1959) noted the high 'correlation' between feeding and *contact comfort* and wondered if feeding really was the important variable in attachment formation, or whether it was the contact which was being confounded with feeding. From earlier observations he noticed that laboratory-reared monkeys became attached to soft, cuddly pads. These observations set up the right conditions for designing an experiment to determine which variable, feeding or contact, was most important in the development of affectional bonds. Box 6.4 summarises Harlow's experiment.

This research study conforms to the essential ingredient of an experiment, which is the production of a comparison while holding other variables constant, and has to be one of the simplest and most elegant experiments ever to be done. It also has had far-reaching impact on child-development research.

Box 6.4 *Love in infant monkeys: a summary of Harlow's experiment*

Aim:	to assess relative importance of feeding and contact in attachment and to develop a testing situation.
Hypothesis:	that infant monkeys attach to cloth rather than wire mothers independently of food source.
Subjects:	Macaque infant monkeys.

Method:

1. Infant monkeys lived in a cage
2. There were two surrogate mothers, one made of cloth, one made of wire
3. Monkeys divided into two groups:
   Group 1 monkeys had a wire mother who also had milk bottle attached whilst the cloth mother had no milk bottle attached;
   Group 2 monkeys had a cloth mother with a bottle attached and a wire mother with no milk bottle.
4. A strange situation test to arouse fear was devised by putting a noisy mechanical toy into the cages.

Measure:	Time spent clinging to mothers.
Result:	Regardless of food source, infants spent more time clinging to cloth mother in the strange situation.
Conclusion:	Contact comfort is a more basic variable in attachment than feeding. Feeding ensures contact. Attachment caused by contact comfort.

Source: Adapted from Harlow, H.F. (1959) 'Love in infant monkeys', *Scientific American*, June. Reproduced with permission

The research environment was carefully controlled to be exact for both groups of monkeys, except for those aspects which were deliberately manipulated to produce the means for comparison – in this case the nature of the food source (wire or cloth mother), and this is the independent variable. The dependant variable, the thing which changes as a result of manipulations and needs to be measured, is the time spent on the mother. Importantly, experimental research, like this, needs to have a hypothesis based on existing theory. In this case, Harlow was testing Freud's assumptions about the role of feeding in the formation of affectional bonds. In fact, Harlow obtained results which are contrary to Freud's less systematic observations of feeding behaviour. The basic design is depicted in Figure 6.8.

In order to test the ethological theory that sensitive caregiving is critical for the development of secure attachments, Ainsworth et al. (1978) observed mothers and infants from birth until 12 months of age. A test of attachment security was devised and conducted at 12 months and correlated with the earlier mothering assessments.

This classic research described by Ainsworth et al. (1978) shows how similarly controlled laboratory experiments can be conducted on human infants whilst at the same time allowing for a degree of naturalistic observation. Strictly speaking, it does not have a control group for comparisons or independent variables. Rather it is better described as controlled observation. The fearful situation devised by Harlow was adapted for human infants by Ainsworth et al. (1978). They wanted to measure human attachment behaviour in an experimental procedure which potentially induces a fear response in the infants. To this end they devised the Strange Situation – a procedure which enables an assessment of the extent to which the infant treats the mother as a source of security in a frightening situation and as a secure base from which to explore novel situations. The Strange Situation takes place in a laboratory playroom where a mother and her 12 month old infant experience a series of separation and reunion events. There is a sequence of eight episodes during which the persons present – mother, baby, stranger – are manipulated. Thirty 12 month old infants and their mothers experienced these

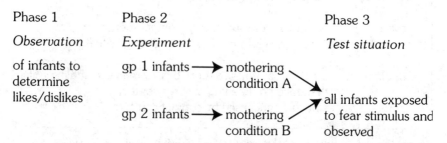

Figure 6.8   *Design overview of Harlow's experiment*

strictly controlled sequences of events, in the same standard environment, with each episode lasting the same amount of time for each mother–infant pair. The experimenter is able to observe and record the attachment behaviour from a one-way window in the playroom. The observer, stranger and mother are each given specific instructions on what to do and how to do it during each episode. Each episode is scheduled to last 3 minutes but may be a bit shorter if a child becomes extremely distressed.

In episode 1 the observer simply introduces mother and infant to the playroom, gives the mother brief instructions, then leaves. The second episode begins when the mother, as instructed, places the infant on the floor to play amongst some toys whilst she sits across the room and reads a magazine. An unfamiliar woman enters and begins episode 3. She interacts with the mother and then attempts to interact with the baby. Episode 4 – a separation – begins when the mother leaves the room and the stranger is non-interactive except to try to comfort distressed infants. The fifth episode – a reunion – is when the mother returns and pauses at the door to see if her infant approaches her. The stranger leaves as the mother tries to comfort the infant, if needed, and to get the infant interested in the toys again. Episode 6 is another separation and begins when the mother says 'bye bye' and leaves the infant alone. The stranger begins episode 7 by entering and soothing the infant if needed. In episode 8, the mother returns and is reunited with the infant.

During each episode the observer is recording the infant's behaviour, noting the use of the mother as a secure base, the infant's exploration of the toys and room and proximity to the mother, the infant's reaction to the mother's departure and return and willingness to explore the room and toys in her absence.

From these controlled observations, Ainsworth et al. were able to classify children according to four observed attachment behaviour patterns.

- Type A children had behaviour patterns described as 'anxious–avoidant'. These infants ignore the mother at reunion or look at her and look away. Typically these infants show no outwards sign of distress even though later research suggests they have an increased heart-rate (Spangler and Grossman 1993).
- Type B infants have 'secure' behaviour patterns. These infants approach the mother upon reunion, are comforted by her and prefer the mother to the stranger.
- Type C infants are described as 'anxious–resistant' (or insecure–ambivalent). They do approach the mother but resist contact with her in reunion episodes, appearing angry or passive.
- Type D infants show a 'disorganised–disorientated' behaviour pattern. They are confused, depressed or dazed upon reunion, perhaps with some contradictory behaviours. Heart-rate is greatly increased, showing intense alarm when the mother leaves (Spangler and Grossman 1993).

A classic experiment, known as The Bobo Doll Experiment, involving children was conducted by Bandura et al. (1963). In order to test their hypothesis that children who are exposed to adults behaving aggressively will score higher on measures of aggression than children not exposed to adults behaving aggressively, they had to design a method of differences. That is, they had to find a way of manipulating levels of aggression, their independent variable, whilst holding all other variables constant. They decided to use a film of an adult behaving aggressively towards a plastic 'Bobo' doll. In doing this they ensured that the stimulus was exactly the same for each child being exposed to it.

Next they decided to have two groups of similar children. One group would receive the independent variable (also known as the experimental condition) and the other would not receive the independent variable (also known as the control condition). To ensure that both groups of children were similar, they would be randomly assigned to each group, rather than say, friends being allowed to go together in one group. Figure 6.9 depicts the design overview of Bandura's experiment.

Survey methods

A commonly used method in education, health and social work research is the *survey*. A broad aim of survey research is to describe what is actually going on, in a particular field of practice, regarding a particular issue of some importance. An example might be finding out what are the policies, if any, of all pre-school providers on the provision of a core curriculum for pre-schoolers. Surveys can tell us about standards for comparing existing conditions and help us in determining the relationships that exist between specific events (Cohen and Manion 1994). Surveys are composed of questionnaires, rating scales and sometimes highly structured interviews. These methods are discussed and explored in more detail in Chapter 7 and practicals. A brief description of the survey as a general method is useful at this time.

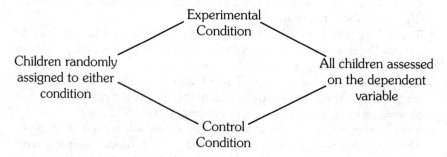

Figure 6.9   *Design overview of Bandura's experiment*

In survey research, a large number of questions are devised into a questionnaire, rating scale or structured interview. The questionnaire can be structured with fixed, alternative responses or unstructured with open-ended questions which allow participants to express their answers in a more personal way. Surveys are designed to be administered to very large numbers of participants who are a representative sample of an even larger population. A survey sent to every social services manager in every local authority in the country, represents the views of the entire population of social services managers in the country.

In an interesting study, Rutter et al. (1979), combined survey methods, structured interviews and classroom observation. The aim of the study, called *Fifteen Thousand Hours*, was to examine how secondary schools in an Inner London Education Area of 6 miles radius differed in terms of academic achievement, attendance and delinquency. Variables considered important for differences included: status and sex of pupils; organisation of school environment (size, space, staff, class size, age and sites of buildings). The survey was conducted on how the twelve schools in the area selected measured up in terms of these variables.

A good example of a questionnaire survey is that of Blenkin and Yue (1994) which produced a profile of early years practitioners as an investigation into the quality of educational provision for the early years in England and Wales. This entailed obtaining information concerning both the nature and quality of provision, including quality of setting, resourcing and qualifications of professionals and others working with the children. Qualitative views of practitioners on what is meant by quality of provision were also obtained. Box 6.5 illustrates their objectives in designing the questionnaire.

Box 6.5　*Objectives for an education survey questionnaire*

- to elicit information on the nature and qualifications of practitioners
- to identify key factors/criteria supporting/constraining curriculum development
- to identify key factors influential in the professional development of practitioners
- to obtain practitioner definitions of quality curriculum
- to obtain practitioners' suggestions for improvements in current educational provision
- to obtain practitioners' suggestions' for improvements in professional training and development

---

Source: Adapted from Blenkin, G.M. and Yue, N.Y.L. (1994) 'Profiling early years practitioners: some first impressions from a national survey'. *Early Years*, 15(1): 13–22. Copyright Trentham Books Limited, 1994. Reproduced with permission

Survey designs like those described above enable you to collect a lot of data very quickly and can cover examination of large amounts of variables. They give good descriptions of the way things are and indicate other possible studies and methods.

Case study methods

What is a 'case' and how is it studied? Our classic idea of a case study is probably exemplified by the work of Freud. Box 6.6 illustrates an extract from Freud's (1909) case analysis of a phobia in a 5 year old boy, Little Hans. Fortunately there are alternative and more modern approaches to case study. More reliable case studies are often used by health practitioners to, for example, monitor the effectiveness of behavioural or medical therapies. Social scientists tend to 'case' study an individual, a relationship, a family, a group, an institution, a work team, a resource or an intervention. Some examples might include: the relationship between a mother and her terminally ill or disabled child; coping with epilepsy at

---

Box 6.6   *Extract from* Analysis of a Phobia in a Five Year Old Boy *(Freud 1909)*

Other observations, also made at the time of the summer holidays, suggest that all sorts of new developments were going on in the little boy.

Hans, four and a quarter. This morning Hans was given his usual daily bath by his mother and afterwards dried and powdered. As his mother was powdering round his penis and taking care not to touch it, Hans said: 'Why don't you put your finger there?
Mother: Because that would be piggish
Hans: What's that? Piggish? Why?
Mother: Because its not proper
Hans: [*laughing*] But it's great fun[1]

1 Another mother . . . told me of a similar attempt at seduction on the part of her three and a half year old daughter. She had a pair of drawers made for the little girl and . . . to see whether they were not too tight for walking . . . passed her hand upwards along the inner surface of the child's thigh. Suddenly the little girl shut her legs together . . . saying: "Oh mummy, do leave your hand there. It feels so lovely."

Source: Freud, S. (1909) *Analysis of a Phobia in a Five Year Old Boy,* Vol. 8, Case History 1. Copyright Penguin, 1977. Reprinted with permission

school, one child's strategies; or a study of a child's care experience whilst mother is in hospital.

A case study is an in depth look at an individual, in context, a situation or an intervention, but each case also has a number of elements within it, which make up a total picture or a vignette which 'says it all'.

An earlier survey on child care workers, which solicits the practices and views of practitioners on the lack of an adequate practice framework for addressing the needs of the children of the mentally ill, can be enhanced by a case study of a family which nicely illustrates the whole situation. If a new practice policy is set up and interventions implemented by way of a special unit, this could be a case study on the process of change, in which views of managers, workers, parents and children are sought. Like survey methods, case studies employ a variety of methods such as observation, questionnaires, standardised assessments, rating scales, in-depth interviews and other data sources such as narratives, texts, documents and reports. These methods are discussed in Chapter 7.

Ethnography

Ethnographers conduct research, usually by participant observation, into all aspects of a culture and have been studying child development in varying cultural and social settings for some time (e.g. Mead and Wolfenstein 1955; Whiting and Whiting 1975; Whiting and Edwards 1988). One study involved research teams in different countries asking similar questions about child-rearing practices and using similar methods across social settings (Whiting 1963). In a sociological study, Leavitt (1996) examined the emotional culture in day-care settings. Methods included participant observation, field notes and a form of analysis which depended on interaction and telling stories in interpreting events observed and experienced.

The emotional culture of settings was experienced through daily practices, regulative norms (such as rules on crying), caregiver beliefs regarding involvement and professional distance; alienation from the child's emotions and the construction of the antiself (in that children's emotions and selves were not given meaning through recognition and response, which leads to a loss of self for the child). As this example illustrates, ethnography is a qualitative research approach which gives importance to the interpretation of actions and the contexts in which they occur. Theory plays an important role in ethnographic research. Existing themes can inform and be tested in this kind of research. Leavitt's research was conducted within a symbolic interactionist framework and interpreted in terms of Marxist theory. Nevertheless, new theory can often emerge from ethnographic field notes, observations and interviews (see Practical 7.5). Box 6.7 lists some of the ethnographic methods used for doing research with children of various ages.

Box 6.7 *Some ethnographic methods used for doing research with pre-schoolers*

For studying the transmission of cultural values: passive participant observation + informal interviews + formal interviews.

For studying spontaneous use of English at home as practice play for peer play at school: narrative play – tape recordings of play sessions of a bilingual child + field notes by the mother.

For studying the social and creative behaviour of four 'highly original' children: observation, video, interviews.

For studying peers constructing their own culture:participant observation of access rituals and friendship and description of field entry strategies.

For studying pretend play: ethnographic interviewing + non-participant observation + analysis of children's writings.

For studying excellence of practitioners working with children: life stories and narrative accounts of several excellent practitioners in different contexts; stories constructed from interviews, participant observation, written correspondence and autobiographical reflection.

Source: Adapted from Hatch, J.A. (ed.) (1995) *Qualitative Research in Early Childhood Settings*. Copyright J. Amos Hatch, Praeger Publishers, 1995. Reproduced with permission

Practical 6.1: Child observation

The aim of this practical is to give you some experience of doing and scoring child observation. It is best done with real children or a good quality video of children interacting. Figure 6.10 shows an observation sheet, designed for event sampling of predetermined categories, in a checklist format. You are required to indicate each incident of each behaviour by entering a tick alongside the observed category. Firstly, examine the coding scheme and ask yourself what you think it is trying to do. Is it a reliable and valid system? How can we find out? Do you anticipate problems? Conduct the observation.

BEHAVIOUR	FREQUENCY										TOTAL
Social:											
interactive											
solitary											
parallel											
Emotion:											
laugh											
cry											
smile											
hits											
comforts											
Cognition:											
questions											
argues											
instructs											
fantasy play											

Figure 6.10   *Observation sheet*

Once you have conducted the observation, ask yourself / discuss with others the following issues:

- What is it trying to do and does it succeed?
- Problems of format/layout.
- What crucial things are missing from the proforma?
- Problems of conducting the observation.
- Can the procedure be improved?
- What do you think of the selection and categories of behaviours?
- How can you improve knowing which behaviours to select?

Practical 6.2: Designing your own observation sheet

The aim of this practical is to promote critical thinking in designing your own observation sheet. Design your own observation sheet for studying target child bullies. In designing it, ask yourself:

- What kind of sampling and recording is best?
- What do I mean by bullying?
- Are there different forms of bullying and if so what are they?
- Who else matters in bullying?
- Do their responses matter and can they be defined and categorised?
- Does it matter how the episode starts and finishes?

Practical 6.3: Assessing validity

The aim of this practical is to explore how to determine validity of child behaviour categories to be observed. Distribute your designed proforma to 10 child experts such as teachers, nurses, psychologists and ask them to rate your categories in terms of your stated purpose.

Practical 6.4: Assessing reliability

The aim of this practical is to explore means of assessing reliability. You have already conducted, coded, calculated and generally assessed validity of a coding scheme. Now you are going to formally assess its *reliability* – that is, assessing the consistency of your coding scheme across two different raters. You will need to co-operate with a partner or group. This can be done informally by assessing the percentage of agreement between you and your co-rater for each behaviour category. Strictly speaking, however, it should be done using a formal correlational test such as *Pearson and Spearman Rank Order Correlation* Test; or, Cohen's *kappa* test.

Together with your partner, follow the steps below:

1 Copy your partner's total for each observation category from your observation practical.
2 Write them into corresponding columns beside your own totals.
3 Calculate percentage of agreement between you on the overall coding scheme. Is it reliable?

If you do not have a partner, re-do the same coding scheme in a few weeks and calculate the percentage agreement between the two observation sessions. This is a form of test – retest reliability.

4 If you feel able, consult a statistical manual and recalculate using one of the tests named above. Which one should it be?

Practical 6.5: Role-play (adapted from Wattley and Müller 1984)

This practical aims to improve self-awareness, the ability to see the world from another's point of view and to appreciate how you are perceived by others. This is an *experiential* practical which has implications for professional practice with children.

Part 1: Portraits (to be done in pairs, discussed in a large group)
Each person in the pair has to write three descriptions of *what a person is like as an individual/professional.* The first description is of him/herself; the second is of his/her partner; and the third is a prediction of how the partner perceives him/her.

- Exchange portraits with partner and compare and discuss evidence for the impressions expressed.
- Group discussion on implication of portraits for professional practice with children.

Part 2: Translations (to be done in small groups)
Each person writes down their best characteristic and passes it on to the next person who 'translates' it into a problem, e.g. 'I am considerate' could become 'You will be put upon with other people's problems'. Then the group discusses all translations and how they came about.

Part 3: Experiential role-play (to be done in groups assigned to different roles)
The class are presented with a disturbing scenario (see Box 6.8) and divided into three groups: group 1 put themselves in the role of the professional involved (this can be education, health or social work depending on group composition), group 2 put themselves in the role of the parent and group 3 put themselves in the role of the child. Each group has to discuss the following issues:

- How do I feel?
- What do I think?
- What can I do?
- What can't I do?

Box 6.8   *A case example*

Molly is 25 and lone parent of two children aged 4 years and 18 months. Her husband left her a year ago, and the children have no contact with him. She is being treated for depression by her GP and is on medication. She has occasional visits from a community psychiatric nurse. She finds it hard to respond to the children, whom she finds fretful and demanding. She shouts at the 4 year old and has told the playgroup leader that she feels at the end of her tether. Molly is on income support. She lives in rented accommodation and is in dispute with the neighbour upstairs about the amount of noise the children make. Her sister lives near but does not help. They have fallen out because Molly borrowed money from her and failed to repay it. The two children have been accommodated by the local authority on two occasions for short periods. Molly talks to the playgroup helper about 'putting them in care' for a break. Today, the playgroup leader phones Social Services to say that the 4 year old has not been picked up from playgroup. She has phoned Molly, who answered the phone but her voice was slurred and she was crying. She said she could not come to get her child and that she has had enough.

One person is nominated from each group to 'act out' their role in what happens next while the other participants become observers. Box 6.9 illustrates some considerations for observers and players. A video tape of the role enactment would be helpful.

Box 6.9   *Some considerations for observers and players in role-play*

Observers

- Pay attention to all forms of communication, including non-verbal interaction and cues.
- Draw up a sketch of what you thought each individual was like as a person.
- Discuss where inevitable courses of action were chosen, possible alternatives and their outcomes.

Players

- How involved did you feel and what problems did you find in playing your role?
- How do you feel about the outcome?
- Go back to crucial points and re-enact an alternative route.

Practical 6.7: Doing an experiment: improving language teaching

The aim of this experiment is to assess the use of keywords or cues in teaching a new language. It is hypothesised that using these 'cues' facilitates encoding of new words which are otherwise meaningless. Table 6.1 lists some Russian/English words and keywords.

Table 6.1   *Russian/English words and keywords*

Russian	Keyword	English
STRANÁ	strawman	COUNTRY
LINKÓR	Lincoln	BATTLESHIP
DÉLO	Jello	AFFAIR
ZÁPAD	zap it	WEST
TOLPÁ	tell pa	CROWD
ROT	rut	MOUTH
GORÁ	garage	MOUNTAIN
DURÁK	two rocks	FOOL
ÕSEN'	ocean	AUTUMN
SËVER	saviour	NORTH
DYM	dim	SMOKE
SELÓ	seal law	VILLAGE
GOLOVÁ	Gulliver	HEAD
TJÓTJA	Churchill	AUNT

Source: Flannagan, C. (1993) *Psychology Practicals Made Perfect – A Level Study Guide*, from Atkinson, R.C. (1975) 'Mnemotechnics in second-language learning', *American Psychologist*. Reprinted with permission.

   You will need two similar groups of people. One group, the experimental group, will be given the keywords (as in Table 6.1). The other group, the control group, will be given the Russian and English words only, that is, no keywords. To improve control, make sure no subject knows Russian and randomly allocate subjects to the two groups (conditions). Allow them ten minutes to learn the Russian words. Then, present them with the English and have them write down the answers. These should be scored for correct responses. Table 6.2 illustrates how to record your data.

Table 6.2   *Recording your data*

Subject	Group 1 (no cue)	Group 2 (cue)
1.	4	9
2.	7	1
3.	10	1
4.	11	8

Table 6.2 *(cont.)*

Subject	Group 1 (no cue)	Group 2 (cue)
5.	5	0
6.	6	2
7.	8	2
8.	11	2
9.	11	2
10.	7	1
11.	0	4
12.	0	1
13.	1	1
14.	1	12
15.	4	4
16.	5	1
Totals (N = 16)	91	51

What is the mean ($\bar{X}$) in each group, where $\bar{X} = \Sigma X/N$?

Group 1: 5.68   Group 2: 3.18

Obviously one mean is bigger, but does it really mean the no cue group learned more easily or is it a chance result?

Describing your data
This exercise will help you to get 'a feel' for the data and to prepare you for the next stage which is statistical analysis. Symbols and formulae often used in journals and research reports are introduced.
   1. From your raw data table, create two new tables (see Table 6.3): one for the experimental group and one for the control group. There should be two columns in each table: one for recording the raw score, in ascending order, and one for recording the number of times that score was obtained (the frequency). Table 6.3 shows you how to describe your data.

Table 6.3   *Describing your data*

Experimental group		Control group	
Raw score	Frequency	Raw score	Frequency
5	1		
6	1		
7	1	7	3
8	1	8	1
9	2		
10	1	10	1
		11	1
		12	1
	N = 7		N = 7

2. This is known as a *frequency distribution* (fd).

3. This data reduction shows characteristics of scores and relationships between the two sets, that is, the experimental group is in the 5–10 range, bunched at 9 (at the end). The control group is in the 7–12 range, bunched at 7 (at the beginning). This retains all the information of the raw data, but is better organised, clearer and more concise. The bigger the data set, the more useful the technique.

4. Calculate the *mean* ($\bar{X}$) of each group: add every score and divide by the total number of scores. Calculate the *median*: rank scores in order of lowest to highest and read off the middle score. Caluculate the *mode*: the most frequently occurring value. Consider the types of data best suited to each of these measures of *central tendency*.

5. Calculate the *mean deviation*, the measure of *dispersion* to reflect the distance of every score/observation from the mean of the scores. In other words, calculate the distance between *each* observation and the mean, and then find the average of all these distances using this formula:

$$\frac{\Sigma \mid X - \bar{X} \mid}{N}$$

where X = any score; $\bar{X}$ = mean of scores; N = number of scores; Σ = sum of; $\mid \mid$ = absolute value of differences.

6. Calculate the *variance* (S^2) or S squared – the number multiplied by itself – which follows the same logic as mean deviation but allows for negative values by squaring the differences:

$$S^2 = \frac{\Sigma (X - \bar{X})^2}{N}$$

7. Calculate the standard deviation (S) which also follows the same logic and is simply the square root ($\sqrt{}$) of the variance, where square root refers to the number which, when multiplied by itself, results in the value of the variance:

$$S = \sqrt{\frac{\Sigma (X - \bar{X})^2}{N}}$$

In order to determine whether the difference between the two means is 'significant' you need to do a statistical test using your raw data. You need a statistics manual to help, or a tutor. If you feel able, you should do a 't' test for unrelated samples or a Mann Whitney U-test, depending on the numbers of subjects in your groups.

7 Special techniques for doing research with children

A number of research techniques have been specially devised for doing research with children. These methods include: developmental tests or tasks; verbal reports either from children themselves or from adults, peers and professionals; and other sources of written information on or about children. These special techniques usually include the likes of questionnaires, interviews, standardised instruments, cognitive and emotional tasks, rating scales, group discussions, reports and records. Correlations between various special techniques and observations are often analysed. In this chapter, we describe some of these techniques in detail.

Developmental test/task performance

In reading research articles on child development you will often come across studies which include one or more tests or tasks for the child participants to do either on their own, with a researcher, with carers, teachers or other children. These tests and tasks have been specially devised by researchers interested in the theory and processes of child physical, social, emotional and cognitive function and development. Whether you are evaluating a task reported in a scientific journal, designing or deciding on a task for your own study, it is essential to consult and keep in mind the theoretical and practical importance of the test or task and the extent to which the performance is a true reflection of underlying biological or psychosocial processes. In the next sections, we describe and discuss a small selection of some of the most frequently used tests and tasks in assessing child physiological, cognitive, emotional and social functioning.

Assessing physiological growth and development

Assessing the child's physiological development entails using both observational and numerical data. A number of behavioural scales have been standardised, that is, based on large surveys of many children to establish developmental norms. These include the Bayley Infant Scales (1969, 1993) and Mary Sheridan's 0–5 years behaviour assessments (1975). Generally, these scales provide an index of the physical and behavioural competences which can normally be expected in early childhood.

Tables 7.1 and 7.2 illustrate the Bayley Scales (1993) and Brazelton

Newborn Behaviour Assessment Scales (1987), respectively. The revised Bayley Scales (Bayley 1993) assess motor and mental development of infants between 1 and 42 months of age and include items on habituation, social referencing and infant memory. Most physiological scales include two subscales: gross motor behaviour; movement of major parts of the body; and fine motor behaviour – small manipulation of hand and fingers, arm control and eye–hand co-ordination. Sheridan includes examination of interactive issues such as play. Table 7.3 shows age norms for the first five years.

Table 7.1   *Example of Bayley Scale item*

Sitting behaviours and efforts to achieve vertical position

Behaviour	Average age (months/weeks)	Age range (months)
(A) Placed by adult		
sits with support	2/1	1–5
sits with slight support	3/3	2–6
sits alone, momentarily	5/1	4–8
sits alone, 30 seconds +	6/0	5–8
sits alone, steadily	6/2	5–9
sits alone, good co-ordination	7/0	5–10

Source: Adapted from Bayley, N. (1993) *Bayley Scales of Infant Development: Birth to Two Years*, 2nd edn. Copyright Psychological Corporation, 1993. Reproduced with permission

Table 7.2   *Example of Brazelton's Newborn Behaviour Assessment Scale item*

Cuddliness

Score	Behaviour
1	Resists being held; pushes away; thrashes; stiffens
2	Resists being held most of the time
3	Doesn't resist, doesn't participate (passive: rag doll)
4	Eventually moulds into arms after lots of nestling and cuddling efforts by examiner
5	Usually moulds and relaxes when first held
6	Always moulds initially as above
7	Always moulds initially with nestling and turns towards body and leans forward
8	Moulds and relaxes, nestles and turns head, leans forward on shoulder, fits feet into cavity of other arm, all of body participates
9	All of 8 plus baby grasps examiner and clings

Source: Adapted from Brazelton, T.B., Nugent, J.K. and Lester, B.M. (1987), 'Neonatal behavioural assessment scale.' In J.D. Osofsky (ed) *Handbook of Infant Development*, 2nd edn. Copyright John Wiley and Sons, Inc., 1987. Reproduced with permission

Table 7.3 *Some age norms for motor behaviour*

Age (approx) years	Gross motor skills	Fine motor skills
3	Balance on one foot (5 seconds)	Copy drawing of a circle
4	Consistently catch bounced ball	Copy drawing of a cross
5	Walk backwards heel to toes	Draw a man with 6 or more parts

Source: Adapted from Sheridan, M.D. (1975) *From Birth to Five Years: Children's Developmental Progress*. Copyright Routledge, 1975. Reproduced with permission

Psychobiological measures

Basic biological measures are increasingly moving out of the specialised fields of paediatrics and nursing and finding a comfortable place in studies on the psychology of behaviour and relationships. Indices of biological and psychological stress are widely used on people and children of all ages. These include measures of blood pressure, heart-rate, skin conductance, stress hormone levels in saliva and blood samples. These sorts of measures have been successfully applied in studies of attachment behaviour in strange situations.

Cognitive tests and tasks

The most commonly used tests of children's cognitive abilities are IQ tests. IQ literally means 'intelligence quotient', and the popular IQ tests of today originated in the work of Binet and Simon (1916/1973). This test and subsequent revisions such as Stanford–Binet, examined a wide variety of behaviours, assumed to indicate intelligence. These were simple tests of the higher cognitive processes such as visual co-ordination, memory, word definition, rather than physiological reflexes, responses and behaviours. Despite tasks such as visual co-ordination (the ability to follow the movements of a lighted match with their eyes and head), the items were generally biased towards verbal behaviour.

Early tests of intelligence arrived at a single score MA (mental age) which described the child's intelligence status. MA was the age at which the child's performance was as good as the average child for that age. If a child passed as many items as the average 8 year old, she would be given a mental age (MA) of 8 years, even if she was in fact 10 years old. This also enables comparison between two individuals the same age. If X has a MA of 8 and Y has a MA of 10 then we know that Y is brighter than X. In making comparisons between children of different ages, the MA cannot tell us which child is brighter, and the IQ or intelligence quotient was devised to solve this problem. In principle, it compares MA and CA (chronological age) and provides an assessment of intelligence that is independent of age. The earlier measure of IQ was achieved by dividing the MA by the CA and multiplying the answer by 100. Box 7.1 shows a worked example.

In the example given in Box 7.1, Anne is functioning at the higher level of 8 as compared with Julia at 6, but Julia is obviously bright for her age whilst Anne is not, and Julia is therefore brighter than Anne. According to Wechsler, however, these calculations can still be misleading. A bright 4 year old with an MA of 6 does not reason in exactly the same way as an average 6 year old. Furthermore, as an average 6 year old, intellectual growth is particularly rapid in earlier years so that a one year difference in MA is not the same thing in pre-school years as compared with older children. These perceptions led Wechsler (1974, 1989, 1991) to devise the *deviation* IQ. In essence it is a more reliable way of comparing an individual child's IQ score against a 'standard'. This standard was obtained by giving the test to thousands of children of varying ages and plotting their scores on a graph to see how the scores are distributed. Most test scores, when plotted in this way, will form a bell-shaped curve, also known as the normal distribution (see Figure 7.1) This means that, in the general population, most children will score within a few points of the mean or average score. The further away the scores deviate from the mean score, the smaller the percentage of children obtaining such scores. Therefore it is reasonable to expect only small percentages of children to obtain scores deviating drastically below or above average.

Box 7.1   *Calculating IQ from chronological age and mental age*

Who is brighter, Anne or Julia?

- If Anne is 10 (CA) with a MA of 8 her IQ is $(8 \div 10) \times 100 = 80$
- If Julia is 4 (CA) with a MA of 6 her IQ is $(6 \div 4) \times 100 = 133$

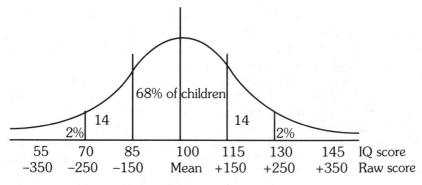

Figure 7.1   *The normal distribution*

Children have an IQ of 100 if their raw score equals the mean score for the children their age in the standardisation sample. Children have an IQ of 115 if their score falls one standard deviation (SD) above the mean for children their age. SD is a measure of variability of the scores. For tests scored in this new way, the average IQ is between 85 and 115 (or the mean of 100 plus or minus one standard deviation) that is, about 68% of those tested will have IQs in the average range.

These tests work well with school-aged children because they are primarily verbal. A different form of test is needed for infants and younger children who have not yet fully developed symbolic verbal expression. Pre-schoolers can be tested on hearing vocabulary, whilst infants can only be tested on sensory, perceptual and motor development and social interactions.

The WISC-R (1974) – Wechsler Intelligence Test for Children

The WISC-R has two measures of IQ. A performance scale has tasks of picture completion, picture arrangement and block design such as the child having to identify what is missing from a picture, reproduce a design, or arrange a series of pictures which potentially depict a story into the right order. The verbal scale tests skills of information (how many fingers do you have?), arithmetic and comprehension (why do we have courts?). This test assesses children aged 5–15 years. The WPPSI (1963) is a version of the test used for pre-school children aged 4–6 years and the WAIS-R or Wechsler Adult Intelligence Scale assesses 16–74 year olds.

Peabody Picture Vocabulary Test – Revised (PPVT-R, Dunn and Dunn 1981) and British Picture Vocabulary Test (BPVT)

These tests are widely used with hard-pressed researchers because they are very quick and easy to do on children of all ages. They do not, however, give an in depth view of individual intelligence. The tester shows the child a series of test plates, each of which shows four pictures of animals, objects, people or situations. The tester presents each test plate of four pictures and says 'show me car' and the child points to the picture. The test words become increasingly difficult such as 'weary' and 'dangerous', and test items are included which even adults do not always get right. This test has instructions for managing young children and produces a hearing vocabulary, standardised score and a mental age (MA) score.

Piagetian tasks

As a theoretician, Piaget was more interested in the cognitive processes underlying task performance. He devised a series of tasks which enabled him to describe the development of cognitive processes such as object permanence, perspective taking and conservation and many others. His investigations enabled him to describe the sequence in which children became accomplished in various cognitive tasks (see Chapter 2). In tasks to assess children's ability to understand *conservation*, the understanding that some property of objects such as number or quantity is not changed by experimenter's adjustments is tested. Figure 7.2 illustrates conservation of number where two rows of coins are arranged so that the two rows are evenly matched in the number of coins and spacing between them. The experimenter then transforms them by pushing the bottom row together and the top row coins apart.

Piaget found that, whilst pre-school children could correctly answer the pre-transformation question 'which row has the most coins?', they consistently failed the post-transformation question 'now which row has has the most coins?', believing that, in this example, there were suddenly more coins in the top row.

These tasks are interesting to researchers for a number of reasons. They illustrate the elegant simplicity of designing tasks for children of all ages, tasks which reveal information about the inner minds of children. Many other researchers have demonstrated how simpler versions of such tasks can be devised, versions more accessible to even the youngest children, and providing evidence that certain abilities are evident much younger than Piaget supposed. Baillargeon (1987) devised a test which strongly suggested object permanence in infants as young as 3 months. Flavell (1978, 1985, 1988) developed simple tasks which illustrate the perspective-taking abilities in 3 year olds. These variations in turn, resulted in the emergence of a new theory, *the theory of mind*, the ability to appreciate the world of mental states such as ideas, beliefs, desires and feelings in self and others and how they may differ. Piaget's tasks have also been methodologically attacked (e.g. Donaldson 1978; Samuel and Bryant 1984) in elegant demonstration of how he underestimated the impact of the social and research context and language used.

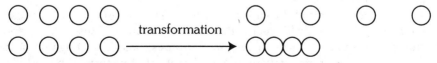

Figure. 7.2 *Piaget's counters or coins task*

Sociocognitive and socio-emotional tasks

Understanding the minds of others

A child possessing a 'theory of mind' has an ability to appreciate the world of mental states, the world of ideas, beliefs, feelings and desires. A task has been developed by Bartsch and Wellman (1989) which demonstrates that 3 year olds have difficulty in understanding the mental states of others. In an everyday situation, if a child is shown a box of chocolates which does not have chocolates inside at all, but instead has marbles in it, he will understand that the box does not contain what he believes it should contain. If the child then sees the box shown to another child who has just arrived, he will believe that the other child, like him, thinks that the box contains marbles. In other words, the 3 year old is unable to attribute a false belief to others.

The task described by Bartsch and Wellman (1989) entails enacting four scenarios with two dolls, depicting situations similar to the marbles in the chocolate box example above. Practical 7.1 describes in detail how to conduct a false belief or theory of mind task on pre-schoolers, and Figure 7.3 shows some video footage of a theory of mind task in process. The basic task design has been replicated and adapted in many research studies. Variations of this type of task have been particularly productive as a tool for researching autistic children and for correlating with task performances in other areas of psychosocial functioning such as attachment (e.g. Fonagy et al. 1997) and with emotion understanding (e.g. Dunn 1995).

Understanding the emotions of others

Denham and Auerbach (1995) devised a task for assessing the ability of pre-school children to understand emotional states of others. These tasks are similar to the false belief tasks in that they use puppets and other props from the world of children in an effort to assess their ability to assess, in this case, feelings from the perspective of the dolls involved, and, in the case of the *false belief* task, the intentions and thoughts of others.

Denham and Auerbach incorporate a well-known simple method of asking young children to either express their own feelings or, in a more complex task, those of others from three faces, made of fabric, wood or paper on which there are three faces drawn, each expressing a different emotion (see Figure 7.4).

Even very young children can use these simple prompts to express their own likes or dislikes and the feelings of others. Researchers ask children to point to faces in response to questions on feelings or post them into boxes or attach them to photographs. In this form, especially in expressing likes or dislikes, it is a form of self-report.

Denham and Auerbach have successfully employed this task in a more

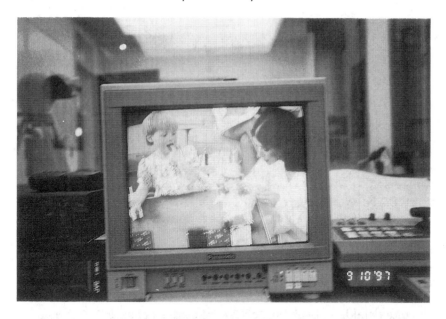

Figure 7.3 *Live video footage of a Theory of Mind Task in progress*

complicated design involving scenarios which evoke the emotions of happiness, sadness, anger and fear. The child witnesses two scenes involving each emotion. In the happy scenes, for example, the puppet is given an ice cream cone and a birthday present. In the angry scenes, another naughty puppet arrives and, in one scene, steals the other

Figure 7.4   *Faces used in an affective labelling task*

puppet's juice/sweets. In the fear scenes, the puppet has a nightmare and witnesses a fire. In the sad scenes, the puppet's best friend goes away and his favourite pet runs away. After each scene, the child is asked how the puppet feels (usually the same sex as the child) and asked to point to or attach the appropriate face to the puppet. The child is given 2 points for each correct answer, 1 point for a correct dimension (a possible answer) and 0 points for each wrong answer. See Table 7.4 for a description of puppet manipulations. Figure 7.5 shows a set of toys especially adapted for this test and some video footage of a child selecting an appropriate face according to the scene depicted by the experimenter. These tasks are becoming widely used in other studies.

In older children, more abstract assessments of children's understanding of emotional states can be done. Gnepp (1989) describes tasks which target a situation where a person's emotion expression is incongruent with what the situation seems to suggest. Children are shown a picture of a girl smiling even though she is about to receive an injection and are asked how she feels. Pre-schoolers would be expected to fail this, whilst 6 year olds may take a reasonable guess at why the girl should be happy. Twelve year olds can do this too, but are also able to perceive the smile as an attempt to hide her fear.

Table 7.4   *Description of puppet manipulations*

Indicators of emotion shown by puppets and puppeteer emotion labelling and situations criterion measures

Emotion	Hand puppet's body language	Puppeteer's facial cues	Puppeteer's vocal tones
HAPPY	'Bounces', spreads arms	Broad smile, wide eyes	'Pearly' relaxed tone
SAD	Wipes eyes, head down	Eyes and mouth down-turned	Whiny, crying tones
ANGRY	Clenched	Eyebrows down, lips pursed	Gruff, growling, clipped, abrupt
AFRAID	Hands up, rigid	Eyes wide, mouth gaping	High-pitched, unwavering

Source: Adapted from Denham, S.A. and Auerbach, S. (1995) 'Mother–child dialogue about emotions and pre-schoolers' emotional competence.' *Genetic, Social and General Psychology Monographs*, 121 (Part 3): 311–37. Copyright Helen Dwight Reid Foundation, Heldref Publications, 1995. Reproduced with permission

Figure 7.5 *Toys and procedures used in the Understanding of Emotion Task*

Understanding conflict

Hay et al. (1992) devised a simple task to assess pre-schoolers' understanding of peer conflict. Two glove puppets – a monkey and a bear (Pat and Terry) – are used as visual aids in the interview. The puppets proceed to have a conflict for the possession of a felt-tip pen; the monkey and bear are randomly assigned to one of the two roles in the conflict for each child. The scenario begins with one puppet, the original possessor of the pen, bringing the pen to nursery and showing it off, noting that 'My father gave me this nice new pen'. The other puppet immediately expresses an interest in the pen and asks to see it. The original possessor refuses and the conflict ensues. The puppet without the pen than grabs for it, and a tussle takes place. Both puppets shout and attempt to gain possession of the pen. The interviewer lets the puppets wrestle then draw apart without the dispute being resolved. In the subsequent interview, the puppets' assigned names are used, after ensuring the child can correctly identify the puppets. The interviewer uses the pronoun preferred by each child (usually male). The child is then asked:

- What does puppet A (initiator) want?
- What does puppet B (protester) want?
- How does A feel (show me)?
- How does B feel (show me)?
- Is this a fight? Why?
- Whose fault is it?
- Who is going to win?
- Who is going to lose?
- If A wants the pen, what should A do?
- What would you do?
- Is there anything A could do that would be wrong?
- If B wants to keep the pen what should B do?
- What would you do?
- Is there anything B could do that would be wrong?
- If they were real people, who would you like to play with?
- Show me how the fight could end.

The Puzzle Task: Observing The ZPD

According to Vygotsky (1978), when children are playing with adults or even older children they are learning how to think (see Chapter 2). The quality of the interaction taking place should, then, tell us something about the quality of the 'scaffolding' children receive from their elders. Nevertheless, the learning process is not entirely in the hands of adults. Children can or should be able to make their own creative contributions to joint activity. The ZPD is the learning zone between a child's actual performance and his potential performance. Obviously not all adults and children are the same regarding the nature of the contributions they make to this learning experience.

The Puzzle Task (Wertsch and Hickman 1987) is a nice example of a task which creates a situation which enables the observation of interaction in the ZPD. Pre-school children and their mothers are given two complete identical puzzles. One puzzle is taken apart and the pair are asked to reassemble it. Mothers are asked to help their child whenever they feel the child needs help. The quality of the interaction can then be assessed in terms of helping the child to understand the task, direct and indirect, referring to the completed puzzle for guidance, the child's contribution to solving the puzzle, e.g. asking questions, and the mother's ability to encourage the child to '*think*' for himself. Two year olds should be able to engage in simple puzzle tasks with a parent, teacher or carer. However, as it is possible to increase the complexity of puzzles, there is potential for similar research on children of all ages. Most recent research continues to find new ways of describing and testing the ZPD (e.g., see Meins and Russell 1997).

Story completion tasks: assessing attachment in pre-schoolers

The Attachment Story Completion Task (Bretherton and Ridgeway 1990) is a way of assessing pre-schooler's quality of attachment to their carers. It involves presenting the child with five scenarios, enacted with hand-held, bendy, realistic family dolls and supporting props. The scenes include, firstly, a training session in which the family celebrate a birthday, and is not assessed. In this scene the tester establishes the nature of 'the game', which is for the tester to start the story and for the child to finish it off. The child is allowed to explore and handle the toys, and the tester can establish an understanding of how to pitch the game and the most effective prompts to use, such as 'and then what happens?' or 'is this story finished now?'. The five scenes include: spilled juice, monster in the bedroom, hurt knee, departure and reunion. Figure 7.6 illustrates the use of family dolls for two of these scenarios: departure and spilled juice.

The issues addressed in story beginnings are: the attachment figure in an authority role; pain as the elicitor of attachment and protective behaviour; fear as an elicitor of attachment and protective behaviour; separation anxiety and coping, and responses to parental return. The child's performance is assessed for security of attachment on all five stories and given an overall classification. Both verbal and non-verbal behaviour is taken into account in terms of appropriateness of content, emotional expression, coherence of story resolution. Box 7.2 describes the procedure and how to classify responses.

The Separation Anxiety Test is an established projective test which classifies the child's responses to a series of photographs or indian ink drawings depicting situations believed to elicit attachment behaviour. Hansburg (1972) produced a version which assesses teenagers and Klagsbrun and Bowlby (1976) adapted this test for use on younger children and pre-schoolers.

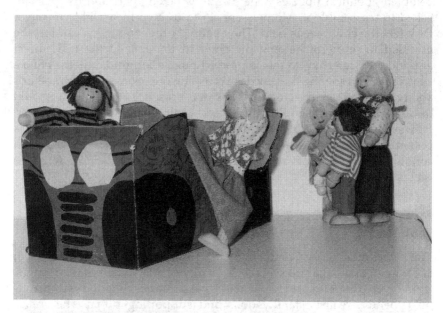

Figure 7.6   *Illustration of doll use in the Attachment Story Completion Task: 'departure' and 'spilled juice'*

Verbal reports

In observing children, the kind of understanding of our participants we gain is about their outer world, that which is acted out and accessible. Verbal reports, however, are research tools which facilitate access to the inner world of our research participants: the world of thoughts, feelings, attitudes and opinions. An often used, if not hackneyed, analogy for conceptualising the many ways in which we can seek to understand these inner and outer worlds of the child, is that of an onion! Large studies using batteries of closed questionnaires are *surveys* which give

---

Box 7.2 *Attachment Story Completion Task*

General props

Two sets of family dolls, each comprising mother, father, male child, girl child. From these sets you need to use one whole family, plus the adult female from the other set as grandmother. Alternate child dolls to suit the sex of the child, i.e. an only boy – use the two male dolls; a girl who has a brother, use one male and one female. For each story begin by saying '*I'll start the story and you finish it.*' Enact your part then say to the child '*Now you show me with the dolls what happens next.*'

Warm-Up (a birthday cake to scale of dolls)

Enact a scene in which the mother produces a birthday cake. There may be some exploration of the toys and it may take a while to make sure the child understands the routine.

Spilled Juice (table, table cloth, bottle of juice, cakes)

Enact a scene in which the child leans over the table and spills the juice. Finish by saying '*Then Mummy says "you've spilled the juice"... show me what happens next.*'

Monster in the Bedroom (no additional props)

Enact a scene where Mummy says '*it's getting late. It's time for your bed*'. Show the child going to his/her bedroom, seeing a monster and shouting '*Mummy! There's a monster in the bedroom!*' from the bedroom.

Hurt knee (piece of green felt (grass) and grey sponge (rock))

Enact a scene where the family go for a walk to the park where there is also a high rock. The child sees the rock and says '*Wow! Look, a high, high rock. I'm going to climb that rock.*' The child climbs the rock and falls off and cries, sobbing '*I've hurt my knee*'.

Departure (Granny joins the family, a box painted as a car)

Enact a scene in which Granny arrives. Then say *'You know what I think's going to happen? I think Mummy and Daddy are going on a trip.'* The parents say goodbye and *'see you tomorrow'* and leave in the car which drives away out of sight.

Reunion (same props as Departure)

Enact a scene in which it is the next day. Granny is at the window and says *'Look children, look who's coming back'*; the car, with parents in, returns.

Criteria for security/insecurity

- *Very secure:* story issues are resolved fluently, without many prompts, and appropriately.
- *Fairly secure:* slight avoidant or odd responses on one or two stories.
- *Avoidant insecure:* don't know or complete avoidance of the issues over three stories or more, even showing some disorganised responses.
- *Insecure disorganised:* odd or disorganised responses over three or more stories even if displaying some avoidant responses.

Source: Adapted from Bretherton, I. and Ridgeway, D. (1990) 'Story completion tasks to assess young children's internal working models of child and parent in the attachment relationship.' In M.T. Greenberg, D. Cicchetti and E.M. Cummings (eds), *Attachment in the Pre-school Years: Theory, Research and Intervention*, pp. 273–308. Copyright University of Chicago Press, 1990. Reproduced with permission

access to the outer layers. Examples might include obtaining details of national or regional policies and practices of managers of child care provision or the opinions of nurses on assessing pain in young children. *Questionnaires* are good for obtaining factual information about the child such as his health history, family status, nationality, number of siblings, age of day care entry. In terms of our onion, this is good surface or outer-layer information. *Attitude scales* delve a little deeper, into the middle of the onion and enable us to assess some aspects of the child's inner world, such as his self-esteem. The real voice of the child, is to be found in the core of the onion and it is the use of special *interview techniques* that will get us there. In the next sections we will consider each of the verbal reports measures, firstly in the form of *other* reports and then in the form of *self* reports.

Other reports

Interviews

A significant amount of what we know about children is gained by well-designed and conducted interviews of adults who know them well – parents, teachers, carers, case workers, health visitors and peers being a few examples. Important issues which potentially influence children via policies and practices can also be examined using interviews. As a method of obtaining the participant's perspective, it has much to offer. Willing participants like being interviewed and the interactive nature of the procedure allows the researcher access to dimensions of information not otherwise available, such as non-verbal cues on feelings. The relatively free-flow interaction enables the researcher to pick up on important and emotive issues by gentle probing and to discover what matters most to the participant from the topics he raises himself. Interviews take time and require detailed analysis, but a well-done interview is well worth it. Table 7.5 offers some general guidelines for designing and doing an interview.

Questionnaires

Questionnaires are a popular research tool because they can be quickly designed, administered – even by post – to large numbers, and are easily analysed. They are often designed by the researcher because their

Table 7.5   *Guidelines for designing and doing an interview*

Designing it	Doing it
• Get ideas on paper, arrange into themes and list in order of intrusiveness	• State purpose, ensure confidentiality and right not to answer and stop at any time, especially if distressed
• Turn into open-ended questions: what? when? how?	• Choose setting carefully for privacy and intimacy
• Ensure questions are clear, unambiguous and short	• Make yourself useful, help in a field setting
• Put in a logical order starting with easy questions, ending with hard ones	• Be interested and non-judgemental
• Avoid leading questions, technical terms, emotive language, negatives	• Tape interview, stick to agenda but allow interviewee some freedom
• End with positive issues/questions	• Techniques to help: expectant pause/ glance; encouraging vocalisations; reflection and returning words used by interviewee; skilful probing
• Pilot interview	
• Re-write	

purpose is to access factual data as it applies to research issues, e.g. questions on practice policies, attendance rates at school, hospital admissions, routines, etc. The design of a questionnaire is similar to the design of an interview, although the administration and nature of data obtained differ greatly. There are, however, a number of standardised questionnaires which are highly popular. One of the most popular forms is for teacher and/or parent assessment of the child's behaviour, also known as the Rutter A and B questionnaires. These questionnaires indicate the extent of behavioural problems, if any. Figure 7.7 illustrates the format of the Pre-School Behaviour Questionnaire. The pre-school version was devised by Blehar and Springfield (1974). For a recent appraisal of these questionnaires see Elander and Rutter (1996). A number of other questionnaires for assessing child behaviour are available such as Achenbach's (1991) Child Behaviour Checklist; Richman and Graham (1971); and the Preschool Behaviour Checklist (McGuire and Richman 1987).

Attitude/rating scale questionnaire

An attitude/rating scale is a special form of questionnaire, composed of a list of statements. Respondents are asked to agree/disagree with each statement on a scale of (usually) 1–5. Figure 7.8 illustrates the format of Abidin's Parenting Stress Index (Abidin 1983, 1995).

	Doesn't apply 0	Applies sometimes 1	Certainly applies 2
16. Tells lies	☐	☐	☐
17. Has wet or soiled self this year	☐	☐	☐
18. Has stutter or stammer	☐	☐	☐
19. Has other speech difficulty	☐	☐	☐
20. Bullies other children	☐	☐	☐

Figure 7.7 *Examples of questions on the Pre-school Behaviour Questionnaire*

Source: Adapted from Blehar, L. and Springfield, S. (1974) A behaviour rating scale for the pre-school child.' *Developmental Psychology*, 10: pp. 601–10. Copyright American Psychological Association, 1974. Reproduced with permission

1 Strongly Agree	2 Agree	3 Not Sure	4 Disagree	5 Strongly Disagree			
1. When my child wants something, my child usually keeps trying to get it	1	2	3	4	5		
2. My child is so active it exhausts me	1	2	3	4	5		
3. My child appears disorganised and distracted	1	2	3	4	5		
4. Compared to most, my child has more difficulty concentrating and paying attention	1	2	3	4	5		

Figure 7.8 *Examples of questions on the Parenting Stress Index*

Source: Adapted from Abidin, R.R. (1990) *The Parenting Stress Index.* Copyright PAR Inc., 1990. Reproduced with permission

The PSI is a popular instrument which assesses a number of different dimensions relating to parenting and the parent–child relationship. There are three broad dimensions of stress: the parent domain, the child domain, and life events and difficulties. The parent and child domain together yields an index of general stress whilst, individually, each domain yields an index of the greater sources of stress arising from the child or parent. The nature of categories within each domain suggests areas which may be considered a 'risk' or 'resilience' factor. Child sub-scales include: adaptability, acceptability, demandingness, mood, distractibility/hyperactivity, and reinforces parent. Parent sub-scales include, for instance, a mother who feels in danger of physically abusing her child may indicate high stress on child distractibility/hyperactivity and positive reinforcement for parent yet indicate low stress in attachment. This could be conceived of as a protective factor, and hypotheses could be generated about the sources of stress and support in general. There are some clinical profiles for child abuse, hyperactivity, disability, and normal pre-school children. For a more detailed guide on attitude measurement, see Oppenheim (1966).

Peer reports/ratings

Children spend a lot of time with peers, in school, in the playground, playing at home. Potentially, then, peers are a good source of information on the behaviour and habits of particular children. One method is to describe specific behaviours to the children and then ask which of their classmates shows the behaviour most often (Masten et al. 1985). The researchers give the interviewee the role of the director of a play, and the cast is made up of children from his classroom. The child is told that, as director, it is his job to choose the right people to be in the play and this means knowing who would be best suited to each role. Roles can be negative and positive representing sociability/leadership, aggressive/ disruptive and sensitive/isolated. Specific characteristics include 'every-one likes to be with' and 'too bossy'. The interviewee nominates children with these characteristics and more than one if several roles apply. In this way, a researcher can discover a child's reputation for aggression, sensitivity, etc.

Another approach to peer assessment of the child's social standing is called *sociometrics*, which could potentially be done in interview or questionnaire formats. A child's sociometric status is an index of social relationships in the form of popularity. These techniques can inform us if a child is popular, rejected, neglected or controversial. Researchers ask all class members to name three children they would most like to play with. These are *positive nominations*. Then the same children nominate the three children they would least like to play with. These are the *negative nominations*. Each child in the class receives a score based on the number of positive and negative nominations received from classmates. These scores are then subtracted to give a measure of *peer acceptance* (positive − negative) and then added to give a measure of *social impact* (positive + negative). These scores can then be further transformed to classify

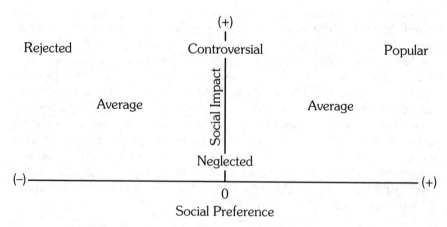

Figure 7.9   *Sociometric status: measuring social impact and social preference*

children into the different categories of social status: popular, rejected, neglected, controversial, average (see Coie et al. 1982; Newcombe and Bukowski 1984). See Figure 7.9.

Although attempts have been made to assess peer status in pre-schoolers using photographs and smiley faces, most successful research of this kind has been done on school-aged children.

Self reports

Interviewing children

Sitting with a child, talking to him, listing to his 'voice' and understanding his perspective is both similar and different to interviewing an adult. What the researcher must bring to both situations is a sense of rapport with the participant, assurances of confidentiality, right to withdraw at any time, and the use of clear, concise questions. In both cases, the researcher needs to be aware of socially desirable responses whilst making the interview an enjoyable and worthwhile experience. From the researcher's point of view, it is important to achieve some standardisation, that is, having elements which are similar for each individual or group interviewed. This will assist in the interview process itself, assuring adequate coverage and facilitating analyses. Consequently, there will be an inevitable tension between covering planned topics and allowing the participants themselves to set part of the agenda. It is a matter of practice and skill that enables researchers to use the interactive quality of the situation to pick up on important issues without pursuing every point raised in detail. On the other hand, children are different from adults, and this makes them special as interviewees and requiring special methods. These methods are qualitative and need to take their competences and motivation into account. The use of familiar settings (home, school) and materials (drawings, games, exercises) allows flexible adaptation to suit the cognitive and linguistic competence of each age group and is valuable in assisting motivation and reducing anxiety. Children respond to the structure provided by visual and verbal prompts, especially in addressing their emotions and their needs. There is, however, surprisingly little guidance available on qualitative interviewing of children.

Obtaining perspectives of children: questionnaires interviewing 5–12 year olds

The general oversight of the usefulness of qualitative methods for doing research with children applies particularly to the 5–12 year old age group. Typically, researchers have focused on pre-schoolers and adolescents because they are presumed critical phases in child development. To this end, Hill et al. (1996) explored qualitative methods which can be used to hear the voices of primary school children. The children's perspectives on their emotions and well-being were explored by adapting qualitative strategies used by practitioners such as social workers and teachers. The result of this research provides an excellent and flexible framework for those who wish to interview children. The paper recommends two principal methods of engaging with children: focus group discussion and individual interviews. The focus group method is good for giving confidence to individuals within the group and allowing the children to set part of the agenda. The individual interview context is, of course, both more private and intimate. It is not difficult to imagine the many research situations in which this approach is vital. Furthermore, used in conjunction with a prior focus group the discussion could go a long way on establishing a rapport with an anxious child via group support, acceptance and an emerging structure of issues to be explored in greater depth with individuals.

The optimal focus group size is five or six, with a small age range, and for some purposes, same sex groups may be a viable option. Children should receive clear explanations of the group's purpose and format with a limited number of themes planned for exploration. Questions should be put in a straightforward open-ended manner, with the provision of a discussion overview from time to time. An important role of the interviewer is to facilitate productive peer interaction for all group members. The discussion agenda set by Hill et al. had the following limited themes: purpose of the research; listing of feelings children have; explaining emotions; the relative importance of different feelings; persistent negative feelings and responses; children's problems and worries; responses by others to children's concerns; adult's feelings and what could promote children's well-being. These group discussions were conducted in the children's schools and individual interviews either at home or in school. The individual interviews used some of the same techniques and emerging themes of the group discussion but were able to explore particular emotions in greater depth with individual children. In this case, the researchers felt the children were more relaxed in the school setting than at home. Table 7.6 summarises the variety of methods used to engage the children in both group and individual contexts. The preferred modes vary according to the age, context and individual child.

It should be noted that group interviews do have some drawbacks. They are difficult to tape record and transcribe (who is saying what?), impossible to record in note form whether you are leading the group or merely observing. Group activity also leads to group effects, with some voices being heard more than others.

Table 7.6 *Methods for obtaining 5–12 year olds' perspectives on their emotions and well-being*

Group interviews

Introductions	Researcher and children make name labels and say a bit on self
Brainstorming	Naming and noting all feelings thought of for discussion focus
Visual prompts	• Outline faces showing different emotional expressions
	• Mr Numb the Alien with no feelings for children to explain meanings of feelings named
	• Pictorial vignettes: four pictures showing two friends fighting and making up (discuss likely cause and resolutions). Picture of a couple rowing while washing and drying up (discuss family tensions)
Role-play	Act out situations where a child is unhappy/fearful/worried and an adult is sought to help. Gives information on typical adult interventions. Needs careful preparation and debriefing
Self completion questionnaires	(work sheet) Gives quantifiable data. Provide help for less verbally articulate children
	Sentence completion: 'I am sad when _____'
	Fantasy wishes: 'List 3 things that would make you happier'
	Simple chart: indicates who the child would ask for help with worries mentioned
Drawing	Entitled 'This is a child who is feeling _____ because _____'

Individual interviews

Introduction	About myself sheet. Likes/dislikes (food, pop stars)
Ecomap	Important people: 'Easiest to talk to', 'best helpers', 'most fun' also used in later discussion on specific emotions noted
Outline faces	As in group
Sentence completion cards	On intense feelings 'I feel really safe when _____', 'the saddest I ever felt was _____'
Role-plays	Researcher pretends to be a child seeking help from a friend: situations extracted from group prior discussion
Questionnaire	As in group

Source: Adapted from Hill, M., 'Laybourn, A. and Borland, M. (1996) 'Engaging with primary-aged children about their emotions and well-being: methodological considerations.' *Children and Society*, 10: 129–44. Copyright John Wiley and Sons, Ltd, 1996. Reproduced with permission

Interviewing children: perspectives on social relationships

Anthony and Bene (1976) devised a technique for the objective assessment of the child's family relationships. The test is designed to give a concrete representation of the child's family. It consists of 20 figures representing people of various ages, shapes and sizes which are ambiguous so that they can be from any family, but also the child's family under suggestion. Each figure has a box-like base with a slit at the top. Cards with character descriptions can be posted into these boxes. Box 7.3 gives examples.

The child selects a figure to represent each member of his family including himself. Then the tester introduces Nobody. This is a character who accommodates 'sentiments' which the child does not want to apply to the Family Figures. The tester then shows the child the cards, explaining that each one has a message on it and the child is asked to post each one into the person whom the message fits best, or into Nobody if it fits none of the family characters.

Standard questionnaire

A good example of a popular self-report questionnaire is Kovacs' Child Depression Inventory or CDI (1981, 1985). Figure 7.10 illustrates some of the items and questionnaire format for assessing the child's current mental state. This questionnaire is designed for use on school-aged children and has been used in a study by Cole et al. (1997). This paper illustrates a number of self and other verbal reports which assess the child's perceptions of peers and self.

Box 7.3   *Examples of 'sentiments' from the Family Relations Test*

This person in the family is very kind hearted.
This person in the family is very nice to me.
This person in the family is sometimes a bit fussy.
This person in the family sometimes nags at me.
I like to cuddle this person in the family.
This person in the family likes to tickle me.
Sometimes I hate this person in the family.
This person in the family makes me feel afraid.
This is the person in the family father pays too much attention to.
Mother worries that this person in the family might get ill.

Source: Anthony, E.J. and Bene, E. (1976) *Family Relations Test.* Copyright 1976 Bene and Anthony. NFER-Nelson Publishing Co. Ltd, Windsor, UK, 1976. Reproduced with permission

Please tick the box ☐ next to the sentence that best describes the way you have been feeling over the past two weeks, including today.

1. I am sad once in a while ☐

    I am sad many times ☐

    I am sad all the time ☐

2. Nothing will ever work out for me ☐

    I am not sure if anything will ever work out for me ☐

    Things will work out for me ok ☐

3. I do most things ok ☐

    I do many things wrong ☐

    I do everything wrong ☐

Figure 7.10 *Examples of questions on the Child Depression Inventory*

Source: Adapted from the Children's Depression Inventory (CDI) by Maria Kovacs. © 1998, Multi-Health Systems Inc. Reproduced by permission.

Other verbal reports

Life histories

What can be learned by listening to one person retell the story of their life? It tells us a lot about that person, about the childhood experiences which have influenced them, and the historical events and cultural contexts which have further shaped what this person has become over the years. Suppose what this person has actually become is a first class case worker with a unique talent for helping to maintain unity of families involving child abuse. Now the life history gives us so much more. For example *what* exactly does she *do* in her daily practice and *why*, where does the skill and motivation come from to be as good at her job as she is? This kind of research opens yet another door through which to enter the world of the child. This one person can enlighten us on how to make the world a better place for children to be in. The stories of such individuals who work with children can inform practice by way of example. They can also make powerful statements about troublesome social, educational or

---

Box 7.4   *Life history: a method for entering and understanding the lives and work of others*

I   Interview participant several times over a year. Seek interviews with key colleagues and relatives.

II Ask questions leading to intersubjective understanding:
   A   What was it like for you to do your job?
   B   How did you come to do your job?
   C   Tell me as much as you can about your life up to the present time.
   D   What is the meaning of what you do for you?
   E   How do you understand it in your life.

III Respond with stories from your own life.

IV Describe your role in the process to improve validity.

V   Get feedback from the participant on your written report.

Source: Seidman, I. (1998) *Interviewing as Qualitative Research: A Guide for Researchers in Education and the Social Sciences*, 2nd edn. Copyright Teachers College, Columbia University, 1998. Reprinted with permission

health issues such as multi-cultural education or maintaining the unity of families involved in child abuse. Research of this kind also recognises and uses the intersubjective nature of naturalistic research. It is worth noting that there are different kinds of stories. A life story is about a life, life history includes information on historical and cultural contexts. A narrative is a way of presenting human actions and events in a meaningful structure. Telling stories is a process of creating meaning from one's past experiences as well as creating meaning for the future. There is also the form of story being told in the report of an interview. Box 7.4 outlines a way of doing life story/history research.

Other narrative forms of research include narrative reports of behavioural observations, and self-descriptions written by practitioners. Life story/history research is demanding in the same way as Tavistock Model observation – a trusting relationship needs to be developed and sustained over a long period of time. Narrative essays can be obtained from children also, and in large quantities if a whole class or school is done at the same time.

Other written sources of information

There is a wealth of existing data which is easily collected and analysed if you know where to look. Organisational policies and practice guidelines, school reports, health records, case notes, samples of children's work, etc.

These can be turned into quantitative data or analysed in the same way as interviews and texts (see Practical 7.5 for an introduction to analysing interviews).

Conclusion

There are many ways of assessing children and creatively using such assessments as part of research, but it is important to consider their original theoretical basis. Is the assessment compatible with what you wish to do both theoretically or practically? Do you think it is a reliable and valid way of making the assessments?

Practical 7.1: Understanding beliefs of others

This practical aims to provide you with experience of conducting a false belief task with children. To conduct this practical you will need:

- approved access to a pre-school child of 3–5 years of age (see Chapter 8 for guidance on ethics);
- two rag dolls – male or female – which are held easily;
- two boxes of raisins, two boxes of fish food, two boxes of sticking plasters and two boxes of crayons. For each pair of boxes, make sure one has a picture of the presumed contents and paint out the picture on the other box.

Remove contents from the boxes with pictures on them.

Procedure:

1 Sit comfortably with the child at a table.
2 Introduce child to the dolls, e.g. Sally and Anne / Bill and Ben.
3 Put the dolls aside/under the table to give impression they are 'away'.
4 Put the first pair of boxes on the table in front of the child and say *'Point to the box you think has got raisins / fish food / sticking plasters / crayons in it?'*.
5 Let the child have a look to establish that the pictured box is empty and the blank box contains the expected contents.

Stage 1: Prediction (getting the child to **predict** where the doll will look)
Say *'Look, here comes Sally. Shall we see if she can find the ___?'*. Place the doll, looking from one box to the other as if 'looking' and say *'Where will Sally look for the ___?'*. Note the child's response. Put Sally away.

Stage 2: Explanation (getting the child to **explain** the dolls' intentions)
Say *'Look here comes Anne now'*. This time show the doll going straight to the labelled box and try to open. Say *'Look, what's Anne doing? What does she think?'*. You may need to prompt a bit by saying things like *'She thinks something doesn't she. . .?'*. Note the child's response. Put doll away.

Stage 3: Prediction

Bring out the third doll. Place it in front of boxes as if looking. Say *'Here comes Bill/Ben. Point to the box you think he will look in'*. Note the child's answer. Put doll away.

Now repeat this procedure for the other three pairs of boxes. The child scores 1 for each correct answer and 0 for incorrect answers.

Questions to ask/discuss after the practical:

1 How did your child's performance compare with that of others?
2 What did you learn about controlling the environment, and the sorts of strategies you need to manage the child's spontaneous contributions?
3 How did you feel doing this task?
4 Why do you think the explanation phase is important?

Practical 7.2: The pre-schooler's view of emotion

This practical aims to provide you with experience of engaging in an emotion task with pre-school children. To conduct this practical you will need:

- approved access to a pre-school child of 3–4 years of age (see Chapter 8 for guidance on ethics);
- materials to make four flannel faces on which the expressions of happy, sad, angry and afraid are drawn;
- a selection of glove puppets, preferably human form, to correspond with the flannel faces.

The Affective Labelling Task The child examines four, handmade, flannel faces on which the expressions of happy, sad, angry and afraid are drawn. The child is then asked to name each facial expression in response to the request of *'show me the ____ face'*. This task can be used:

- to determine the child's basic understanding of emotion expressions;
- to determine the child's own feelings;
- as a training exercise as part of further tasks or tests;
- to be incorporated into further tasks which clarify the child's understanding of the feelings of others or to clarify the child's own feelings about a person or situation (see example below).

The Affective Situation Task This explores the child's own knowledge of others' feelings in situations that elicit clear emotional reactions such as happiness at being given an ice-cream cone or fear at having a nightmare. Puppets enact eight such vignettes, accompanied by the puppeteer's standardised vocal and visual emotional cues. The child is asked to affix one of the (above) four flannel faces (happy, sad, angry or afraid) to the puppet in order to show how the puppet feels. The protagonist puppet is the same sex as the child. See Table 7.4 for a description of puppet manipulations.

Practical 7.3: Attitude rating scales

This practical aims to provide experience of completing an attitude rating scale and describing the results. The instrument chosen is on a five-point scale from strongly agree to strongly disagree (see Figure 7.11) The practical can be done as an individual and then comparisons made with colleagues. This practical has been adapted from Wattley and Müller (1984), with permission.

Complete the questionnaire below. This will give you an indication of your own attitudes, at a glance, towards mildly and severely mentally retarded children. Do you detect any differences in your attitudes to each group? What profile have you given to each group? Is it possible to 'get a feel' for these questions by simply glancing at your responses. However, it is possible to be much more precise in describing these differences and profiles by converting responses into numerical data. To do this:

1 Count the total number of colleagues choosing each answer.
2 Add agree and strongly agree to create one category 'agree'. Add disagree and strongly disagree to create one category 'disagree'. You now have three categories (agree, uncertain and disagree) for each group (mildly retarded and severely retarded).
3 Tabulate your results (see Figure 7.12).
4 Now you can consider differences in attitudes towards mildly and severely retarded children amongst your colleagues. If your colleagues are divided on professional interests, say education, health and social welfare, it should be possible to record data separately for each professional group and to consider differences in attitudes between professionals.
5 It is also possible to obtain an overall attitude score on each questionnaire which indicates the extent to which either positive or negative attitudes are held towards each group. To do this, you need to convert your original responses into numbers. Each question's response is given a score ranging from 1 to 5; 1 represents the most negative response and 5 the most positive. For the negatively worded questions (1, 3, 4, 6, 7, 10 and 13) the responses score 1 for 'strongly agree' to 5 for 'strongly disagree'. For the remaining questions (2, 5, 8, 9, 11, 12 and 14), the responses score from 5 for 'strongly agree' to 1 for 'strongly disagree'.
6 Final scores on each questionnaire range from 14 (extremely negative) to 70 (extremely positive), that is from a mean score of 1 to a mean score of 5.
7 Calculate each individual's score and add them all together. Divide the new score by the number of subjects to get a mean score for your sample of colleagues and/or various groups of colleagues.
8 What is the mean score for attitudes towards mildly retarded children? What is the mean score for attitudes towards severely retarded children? Is there a clear difference between the means and also between the means of different professional groups if this was calculated?

Please circle the one response which best expresses your agreement or disagreement with each of the items shown for both mildly and severely retarded children. Key: SA = Strongly agree; A = Agree; U = Uncertain; D = Disagree; SD = Strongly disagree

		Mildly retarded	Severely retarded
1.	Special classes are justified.	SA A U D SD	SA A U D SD
2.	Normal children also benefit by integration into regular classes.	SA A U D SD	SA A U D SD
3.	Integration leads to negative behaviour in 'normal' children.	SA A U D SD	SA A U D SD
4.	They should go to special schools where 'normal' children do not go.	SA A U D SD	SA A U D SD
5.	These children would learn more if integrated into normal classes.	SA A U D SD	SA A U D SD
6.	The presence of these children in regular classes impedes the progress of 'normal' peers.	SA A U D SD	SA A U D SD
7.	They may reach their potential but not the level of their 'normal' peers.	SA A U D SD	SA A U D SD
8.	They should not be placed in institutions.	SA A U D SD	SA A U D SD
9.	Integration into regular classes will improve acceptance by 'normal' peers.	SA A U D SD	SA A U D SD
10.	They will feel inadequate in regular classes.	SA A U D SD	SA A U D SD
11.	They have a right to public education.	SA A U D SD	SA A U D SD
12.	Transfer to regular classes creates no problems other than the need for resource teachers.	SA A U D SD	SA A U D SD
13.	They are more likely to be a discipline problem in normal classes than special classes.	SA A U D SD	SA A U D SD
14.	They can learn to live normal lives.	SA A U D SD	SA A U D SD

Figure 7.11   *A rating scale*

Source: Adapted from Siperstein, G.N. (1979) 'A scale for measuring (parents' and teachers') attitudes towards mildly and severely mentally retarded persons'. Unpublished manuscript, University of Massachusetts, Boston, 1979. Reprinted with permission

Number of colleagues selecting each response category for mildly and severely retarded children:

Question	Mildly retarded			Severely retarded		
	Agree	Uncertain	Disagree	Agree	Uncertain	Disagree
1	10	0	5	15	0	0
2	10	1	4	0	3	12
3	0	6	9	8	4	3
↓						
14						

Figure 7.12 *Organising rating scale data*

Source: Adapted from Siperstein, G.N. (1979) 'A scale for measuring (parents' and teachers') attitudes towards mildly and severely mentally retarded persons'. Unpublished manuscript, University of Massachusetts, Boston, 1979. Reprinted with permission

---

Practical 7.4:   Professional care as mothering

The aim of this practical is to develop skills in designing instruments and methods introduced earlier in the chapter and in describing the results. It also creates the opportunity to consider relevant theory and consider the application of a qualitative framework.

There are many professional situations where a child is removed or has to be apart from the biological mother: the special care baby unit at a hospital; the foster placement of an abused or neglected child; or, pre-school provision for the young children of full time working mothers. Situations like this raise many concerns for practitioners with respect to their abilities to be effective substitute mothers to the children in their care. Indeed, is substitute mothering essential for quality care?

To conduct this practical you will need a partner/colleague who is willing to be your participant. The participant should have had actual or similar experience of one of the situations described above. Alternatively, your participant should be able to *imagine* that they have experience of one of these situations. The objective of this 'study' is to *explore* the theme 'professional substitute mothering' and quality of care. You are required to use three different methods:

- life history
- questionnaire
- semi-structured interview.

Consult the main text for a general description of each method. For guidance on interpretation of data, see below.

1 *Life history* Plan and conduct a life history interview with your participant. Try to explore the theme of his/her definitions of quality care in mothering and in professional practice.
2 *Questionnaire* Design and have your participant complete a questionnaire. It should offer a description of demographic details of the professional provision. Examples of these might include: years as a carer; training experience and qualifications; number and ages of children in care; professional responsibilities; practice policy; and background details. Attitudes to child care could be discussed on a scale, that is, a series of statements for the participant to agree/disagree with: 'I think my role is to be like a mother' – strongly agree, agree, uncertain, disagree, strongly disagree. Try to develop the theme of defining quality mothering and quality care.
3 *Semi-structured interview* Issues raised from the life history and questionnaire can help identify the focus of the interviews. Questions need to be open-ended, e.g. 'How do you feel about the children in your care?', 'What do you want to offer them?', 'In what ways do your feelings for the children in your care differ from your feelings for your own children?'. Have topics set which you wish to cover, with these questions: the participant's relationship with the children in care and their parents; the impact of this kind of work on the participant's family; sources of stress and satisfaction.
4 Summarise data of questionnaire and transcribe all interview data.

Practical 7.5: Analysing and interpreting the contents of your written narratives/reports or transcript

The aim of this practical is to introduce you to basic principles of grounded analysis of transcripts. All transcripts from Practical 7.4 should be analysed as described below.

Any written text arising from interviews, observational field notes and other documentary sources are in a form which can be subjected to a *content analysis*. This type of analysis assumes that the emerging language can reveal meanings, priorities, understandings and ways of organising and perceiving the world. In approaching this written data, you will be guided by your research questions, but Charmaz (1995) also recommends asking the following questions: *What is going on? What are people doing? What is the person saying? What do these actions and statements take for granted? How do structure and context serve to support, maintain, impede or change these actions and statements?*

Table 7.5 (see p. 127) and Figure 7.13 provide a summary guide for designing, conducting and coding interviews. These are based on the grounded theory approach of Glaser and Strauss (1967) and content analysis (Babbie 1979).

Phase 1 – Total immersion in the data

In addition to interview transcripts, notes made during or after the interview are useful. These and transcripts should be read and re-read, enabling you to enter the world of the participant and give you a real feel for the data and the interviewee. These first readings should enable you to make notes on the emerging frames of reference of the interviewee: e.g. 'there's a lot of talk about own early experiences of separation from the mother; a lack of professional training on relationship management seems to be a major dimension'. Photocopy all transcripts for coding and preserve originals.

Phase 2 – Headlining

In the way that a newspaper headline sums up the contents of an article, your next task is to re-read the interview and headline all important issues emerging whilst ignoring meaningless data. Headlines or headings should be freely selected at this stage. See Figure 7.13.

These headlines can then be reduced by collating them under broader *categories*; e.g. lack of support, gap in knowledge, lack of training could all be categorised under Training Policy Issues. Each transcript is coded and data reduced into these broader categories to end up with a final list of categories.

Phase 3 – Quality control check

The aim of this phase is to ensure the validity of your categories. This is done by having at least two other people to generate a list of categories without knowledge of the original list. Discrepancies can be discussed and amendments made as a result of this exercise.

Phase 4 – Coding

As you are about to attack the transcripts it is wise to have several photocopies. The original interview needs to be preserved to provide the context. Colour highlight pens can be used to indicate the various categories. Go through the/each transcript and highlight each category. Cut the transcript up and collate all statements together which have been coded in the same category. When collating and interpreting items in each category be sure to refer back to the original transcript and recode to maintain a sense of the whole context. Another important part of the writing phase is using existing literature relevant to the topic being raised. The interview might be reported and illustrated separately from a section which links the findings to existing literature. Or, the literature can be included with the findings to illustrate similarities and differences as the writer goes along.

Interview	Headings
I do see them as my own children, it's one of the reasons I do it but how do I know that's what's best? Nobody shows you how to do it.	• Relationship with child • Motivation • Gap in knowledge • Lack of support, advice and training

Figure 7.13 *Organising a transcript into themes*

PART III

SPECIAL ISSUES

8 Ethics in researching children

Professionals who work with children learn many skills as part of their initial training, through working alongside more experienced practitioners, by reflecting upon each new situation they encounter and in many other different and diverse ways. The difficulty for the would-be researcher who wishes to learn research skills is that opportunities for observing experienced researchers in practice are few and far between. Research in itself can be a time-consuming and lengthy process. A great deal of the development of research design involves cognitive rather than overt behaviours, and the very nature of the researcher–subject relationship often makes it undesirable, if not impossible, to have an outsider present. Such intrusion can influence the research milieu, can be restrictive and can potentially have an effect on the internal validity of the research.

Ensuring that the process of undertaking research adheres to sound ethical principles is part of the general repertoire of skills which the novice researcher will find it difficult to observe or indeed practice. Inexperienced researchers can practise designing interview schedules or questionnaires, they can rehearse their questioning techniques and enhance their powers of observation, but equipping themselves with a repertoire of skills which will prepare them for the ethical dilemmas they might meet when undertaking research with children and their families is much more challenging. It can be argued that ethics is the one part of the research process that should *never* be learned in practice and that the would-be researcher should have ensured that all the potential ethical dilemmas have been considered prior to embarking upon the research. This is true to some extent but careful planning can fail, particularly when human subjects are involved. When those human subjects happen to be children the unpredictability factor rises steeply!

This chapter will therefore explore how the novice researcher can be prepared for those ethical challenges which might occur during the process of undertaking research in practice. As we have said previously this is a practical text, and we will endeavour to explore how the researcher can best be prepared for the unexpected, giving examples from our own experiences and the experiences of others. Before we embark on this exploration, however, it is important that we examine the ethical principles which should underpin the preparation of our research. This examination inevitably includes looking at the foundation of contemporary ethical principles in research and at the differences which exist between professional groups, particularly in relation to the direct involvement of children in research. We consider that regardless of these differences all professionals undertaking research work with children should embrace and adhere to the strictest of ethical codes even though they may disagree about methods. The practical at the end of this chapter asks you to consider this point in relation to your own profession so that you can make up your own mind.

Basis of contemporary ethics in research with children

The study of ethics in relation to research with children involves an underlying knowledge of both general ethics theory and exploration of the general principles of undertaking research on human subjects. This is necessary because the study of ethics in research involving children has only recently (in relative terms) been the subject of debate and discussion in the literature, leaving us to draw upon more general theory which can be applied to children. This apparent lack of specific application to children is, without doubt, partially attributed to the place which children have held in society (see Chapter 1). As we have discussed previously, it is only within the last decade or two that societies have come to appreciate and recognise that children have rights which are specific and which dictate that they should be consulted in matters which affect them.

A useful starting point in this discussion on the ethics of research involving children is perhaps to focus more broadly on the general value of research to the human race. It is all too easy to focus on the grave errors of the past and not to dwell, albeit briefly, on the positive. Beauchamp and Walters (1989) remind us, for example, that all of us who are alive today owe that life or the quality of that life to our ancestors who were prepared to participate in research. The wide use of antibiotics and other medication, the successes of surgical intervention and organ transplantation, and the development of modern cancer treatments are evidence of earlier participation in research by human subjects.

The ethical principles, as defined by Beauchamp and Walters (1989), of autonomy, which is *personal rule of the self by adequate understanding while remaining free from controlling interferences by others and from personal limitations that prevent choice* (p. 28); of beneficence, which requires that as professionals we do no harm and that we assume *an obligation to weigh and balance benefits against harms, benefits against alternative benefits, and harms against alternative harms* (p. 32); and of justice, which is treating the person according to *what is fair, due, or owed* (p. 32) – these are principles which, it could be argued, have relevance to our behaviour as moral human beings in all aspects of our personal and professional lives. In terms of undertaking research involving human subjects, clearly we should act with morality and should not suppose that putting on a label which calls us *researchers* gives us licence to act in any way which is not moral. So why then did it become necessary to develop ethical codes which govern the way in which we undertake research? The simple answer is that abuse of the principles which guided research necessitated its regulation so that there should no longer be any room for subjective interpretation of what is or is not moral. Much of this abuse occurred in Nazi Germany during the Second World War and was brought to the attention of the world during the Nuremberg Trials. The messages which emerged were clear according to Müller-Hill (1992: 48) when writing about the ethical implications of Nazi experimentation:

> The attempt of science to provide acceptable values and ethics has failed. Medicine and science should never again be trusted when they promise to deliver their own ethical values; these values have to come from other sources.

The view that scientists should not self-regulate in relation to ethics and research involving human subjects was founded on the notion that the so-called scientists involved in experimentation during the war were not *monsters or madmen* (Vigorito 1992: 11) but were, according to Katz (1992), part of a regime where obedience was paramount, and where the superiority of the Aryan race was not questioned. Experimentation was aimed at advancing knowledge for the benefit of the Aryan community (a kind of warped and misguided beneficence) but at the expense of adults and children who were considered inferior. It is proferred, for example, that Mengele, who undertook experiments on 1500 sets of twins (including many children), was interested in discovering the secrets of multiple births (Vigorito 1992) so that what was thought of as the superior race could be multiplied at twice the natural rate, and that he was also interested in discovering the hereditary basis of behaviour and physical characteristics (Segal 1992). His methods were torturous, inhumane and frequently resulted in the deaths of the twins.

The value of such research must be questioned, and debate continues as to what should be done with data from these and other experiments. Kor (1992), a survivor of the twin experiments, who was liberated from Auschwitz-Birkenau in January 1945 suggests that because the experiments were unethical the use of data is also unethical. She also warns doctors and scientists in a way which is far more direct than any of the ethical codes in existence, by urging them to take the following pledge:

1 To take a moral commitment never to violate anyone's human rights and human dignity.
2 To promote a universal idea that says; 'Treat the subject of your experiments in a manner that you would want to be treated if you were in their place'.
3 To do your scientific work, but please, never stop being a human being. The moment you do, you are becoming a scientist for the sake of science alone, and you are becoming the Mengele of today. (Kor 1992: 7)

Regulation of research activity

Following the Second World War and the Nuremberg Trials there was shock at what had happened under the guise of this umbrella term called research as well as determination that such atrocities should not occur in the future, resulting in various forms of governance and regulation which are briefly discussed below. Whilst children do not form a discrete group within this governance they are clearly part of the overall concern. From the Nuremberg Trials conducted, following the war, between October 1946 and April 1949 emerged the *Nuremberg Code* which stated certain moral, ethical and legal principles relating to research involving human subjects. The *Code* includes details relating to the necessity for voluntary consent of research subjects, the need to ensure that the research is for the good of society, that designs should have been previously tried out on animals and that unnecessary physical and mental suffering should be avoided. It also refers to the need to assess risk and the rights of research subjects to withdraw from the experiment if they wish, as well as stating that the researcher should be scientifically qualified to undertake the experimentation.

The *Geneva Conventions* of 12 August 1949, and in particular the fourth Geneva Convention, formed an addition to international law in relation to civilians. The original convention of 1864 only applied to combatants as did the Regulations concerning the Laws and Customs of War on Land, annexed to the *Fourth Hague Convention* 1907. The general provisions of the *Geneva Convention Relating to the Protection of Civilian Persons in Time of War* make important statements both about research and about children. Article 14 necessitates the setting up of safety zones, during hostilities, to protect children under the age of 15 and mothers of children under the age of 7 years, and Article 82 states that during internment children and their families should be lodged together to enable them to lead *a proper family life* (International Committee of the Red Cross 1949: 184), whereas Article 147 prohibits *wilful killing, torture or inhumane treatment, including biological experiments* . . . (p. 211).

Some fifteen years following the publication of the *Geneva Convention* and the *Nuremberg Code*, the *Declaration of Helsinki* outlining recommendations to guide physicians in biomedical research involving human subjects was adopted by the World Medical Assembly in Helsinki in June 1964. It was later amended by the 29th World Medical Assembly in Tokyo, in 1975, by the 35th World Medical Assembly held in Venice in October 1983 and by the 41st World Medical Assembly in Hong Kong in 1989. The *Declaration of Helsinki* provides a standard of international ethics in research involving human subjects and, whilst it reinforces the details contained within the *Nuremberg Code* and indeed elaborates and clarifies, it also examines the issue of children as research subjects in relation to informed consent. The *Declaration* discusses that not only should the informed consent of the child's legal guardian be sought but that where a minor child is able, the informed consent of the child should be sought *in addition* to that of the legal guardian. The issue of informed consent is discussed in more detail in the following section.

The *United Nations* was set up and had its charter adopted in 1945, following the collapse of its predecessor *The League of Nations* at the beginning of the war. It made provision for the establishment of a Commission on Human Rights (Dimond 1996a) which set out to prepare an International Bill of Rights (later called the *Universal Declaration of Human Rights*) following the General Assembly of the United Nations in 1948. Within the United Nations family are a number of specialised agencies which have relevance to research involving children, including the *United Nations Educational, Scientific and Cultural Organization* (UNESCO) and the *United Nations Children's Fund* (UNICEF). The *Universal Declaration of the Right of the Child* first declared in 1959 sets out the fundamental human rights to which every child is entitled (see Taylor 1997).

In addition to the charters and conventions mentioned above, a number of professional groups have established their own international and national codes which aim to regulate research within professions, e.g. British Psychological Society (1991), National Children's Bureau (1993). Clearly there are too many to mention within the confines of this chapter but professionals and students hoping to enter the professions should be conversant with their own particular international codes as well as those which directly provide governance within their own countries.

Clearly the unethical experiments which were carried out during the war are extreme examples and we could argue that they have little bearing on our behaviour today. The point which is important and which is alluded to above by Kor (1992) is, however, that all researchers are potentially in a position of power and that power carries the potential for abuse. The relative power of adults to children makes this a double-edged sword when involving children as research subjects. Whilst there are varying extremes to which this abuse can exist it is always important for researchers to consider the potential ethical implications of their work and to ensure that they are guided by the ethical principles we have referred to above. This applies not only to those who are carrying out medical research, but to all researchers. There are rules, although they are not always particularly clear, relating to medical research, but researchers from other professional groups do not have such widely established regulation. Nor would they welcome such restriction. According to social researchers Morrow and Richards (1996), and Hood et al. (1996), the regulation which exists for medical researchers restricts the way in which researchers are permitted to seek the views of children and involves *by proxy* methods (that is asking relevant adults about children rather than asking the children themselves unless there is no other way to obtain the relevant knowledge). Hood et al. (1996) are doubtful of this approach, stating categorically that *research should be not on children but with them and for them* . . . (p. 119). They feel that there is no other way for the voice of children to be heard (see also Chapters 6 and 7).

The debate about whether children should be directly involved in research is one which we wish to highlight rather than continue. What we do firmly believe, however, is that there are commonalities between the professions in terms of the need to gain access to children (either *by proxy* or directly), that informed consent should be sought (from children where possible as well as from significant adults) and that the ethical principles of autonomy, beneficence and justice should be adhered to. A useful way of ensuring that you have considered all the ethical implications of an investigation is to identify *all* those who are involved in the study, including controls and those who are not directly being studied (such as, for example, the siblings of children who are the actual research subjects) and to go through each ethical principle with each person to ensure that all risk has been identified. It is useful during this process to collaborate with a more experienced researcher who is not involved in the particular study but who has some expertise in the area of investigation. This will facilitate your reaching an objective viewpoint before you attempt to gain access. We will discuss this further, later on.

Informed consent

As we mentioned above, one of the common factors in all ethical considerations, including regulatory frameworks, is the need to gain informed consent from research subjects. This means ensuring that they *know* that they have the choice as to whether to participate in the research (in other words that they are true volunteers), that they *know* that they have the right to withdraw from the research at any time if they so wish without detriment to their care, and that they *know* exactly what their role in the research is (that is, what they must do if they choose to participate). This should involve appropriate advice which is relevant to the person's understanding of the consequences of their participation. For example, if participation involves taking a new drug they should be informed of the potential side effects of taking the drug. They should also be told in a way which leaves no uncertainty about what will happen to the results of the research. They need to be aware that it may be published and who will ultimately have access to it. We have seen a few examples when reading student dissertations of where written consent has been obtained on a form which promises that subject's names will not be used and confidentiality and anonymity will be upheld, but because of our local knowledge and involvement in early years practice we have been easily able to identify participants. In some cases it has been necessary, because of the potentially harmful effects of placing certain information in the public domain (such as the library and/or through publication), to restrict access to the final product. In relation to children who are involved in research and informed consent, as we have mentioned earlier the consent of the child and the adult or adults who have parental responsibility should be sought. Dimond (1996a) outlines the basic principles on consent to treatment in relation to children, and discusses that, whilst this is not the same as consenting to participate in research, similar considerations should prevail. Under the *Family Law Reform Act* of 1969 children aged 16 to 17 years old are presumed to be competent to consent to treatment *unless there is a reason to suppose that they are not* (House of Lords, *Select Committee on Medical Ethics* 1994: 15).

Under the *Children Act* of 1989 (Department of Health 1989) children under the age of 16 years may consent to treatment if it can be shown that they have sufficient understanding and intelligence to understand fully what is proposed (House of Lords, *Select Committee on Medical Ethics* 1994). Dimond (1996a) suggests that it is advisable to obtain parental consent in addition to the consent of a child who has been shown to be legally competent. There is, however, a potential anomaly which relates to refusal to consent as discussed by the *Select Committee on Medical Ethics* (1994), which states that *the right of minors to refuse consent has not been upheld by the courts* (p. 15). It is suggested that denial to allow *refusal* to consent in many ways denigrates the right to *give* consent as they exist on the same continuum.

There is also a distinction in health care research between consent to what is described as therapeutic research as opposed to non-therapeutic research. Therapeutic research is where there will be direct benefit to the subject which relates to his or her medical treatment (Dimond 1996b), whereas in non-therapeutic research there is no direct benefit to the subject. An example of therapeutic research would be the investigation into the optimum wearing time of wet wraps for children with eczema because the child has eczema and may benefit from the research, whereas a study which undertook ultrasound examination on the abdomens of healthy new-born infants would be classed as non-therapeutic, even though other non-healthy babies may ultimately benefit. Dimond (1996a) suggests that non-therapeutic research should only be undertaken if the risk to the child is *negligible* (p. 177). The researcher must make the decision as to what negligible may mean within any given context. In terms of medical research this process is perhaps simpler than in psychological or social research, where the risks may not be as obvious. For example, if healthy children are subjected to having blood samples taken it will inevitably involve some pain, however transient, for the child and the risks are fairly obvious. On the other hand, interviewing a group of adolescents about parasuicide may have more covert effects, and the risks are not so apparent.

One final note in relation to our discussion about informed consent is the issue of research designs which involve *covert participant observation* (see also Chapter 6). In this type of research the researcher may undertake observation without informing his or her research subjects that the observation is taking place. This is justified (or otherwise) on the basis that, if the subjects are aware that they are being observed, they may change their behaviour and thus the researcher would not gain a true and accurate picture of normal behaviour. This is described as the *Hawthorne effect*. This type of research clearly raises concerns about consent since direct consent from those who are being observed is not possible, otherwise they would know that they were being observed. The important issue here is whether others have the right to give consent for such covert activity to take place. Arguably it is not right because it breaches all codes which clearly state that informed consent should be obtained. On the other hand it is perhaps more important to consider the context of the research problem and to identify the risks and the benefits.

Gaining access

It might perhaps seem strange to discuss gaining access after our discussion about informed consent, rather than before. However, our reasons for doing this are because issues of informed consent should be considered prior to gaining access, mainly because those people whom you will approach to gain access will wish themselves to be informed as to how you intend to gain consent from either the child, the parents (or those with parental responsibility) or both. They will also wish to see copies of intended letters or forms which you intend to send or issue to subjects to gain their written consent.

Gaining access to research subjects and/or research sites requires approaching what are known colloquially as *gatekeepers*, who are defined by Hek et al. (1996) as *people who are attempting to safeguard the interests of others* (p. 73). Among the most important and established gatekeepers in terms of gaining access to sick children is the *Local Research Ethics Committee* (LREC), established by the Department of Health Guidelines (DoH 1991), but existing in a similar format prior to that time. The LREC is a District Health Authority body rather than belonging to a single National Health Service Trust. The LREC is established to provide a committee review and comprises at least two lay members (usually members of the church), and should also include a nurse representative in addition to medical personnel. Pickering (1996) states that all research which is carried out on NHS premises, or which involves NHS patients or records should first gain the permission of the LREC.

The process of gaining consent from a LREC should not, however, be underestimated. Our own experiences show that committees operate in very different ways and to different time scales. We have come across examples of committees which only meet four times per year, and with a very full agenda meaning that your particular proposal may be postponed until a subsequent meeting (meaning a potential 6 month delay in gaining approval). Others provide complex structured forms which need to be produced for each member of the committee (sometimes ten or more members). Again our experience with these forms shows that they are adequate *if* you wish to undertake a randomised controlled trial but are totally inappropriate if you are intending to undertake a qualitative study, using for example a focused interview as your data collection method. Our experience has shown that it is possible to work with LRECs and indeed they can be extremely positive. One chairman we know admits that his personal experience of qualitative methods is limited but acknowledges the importance of all approaches to research. It is almost always useful to have informal discussion with the chair prior to submitting a written proposal, particularly if your intended study doesn't fit the mould of traditional, positivistic research. Other important gatekeepers are those people who manage the research site or access to those people who are your intended subjects. Again these people can be extremely helpful and good communication with them is a prerequisite to success. For example, Ersser (1996) discussed the helpful relationship he established with the ward sisters and doctors who were the gatekeepers in his ethnographic study. On the other hand, Hood et al. (1996) experienced difficulties with their gatekeepers, necessitating a change in approach. Their description shows a similar frustration felt by many:

> We originally planned to obtain the majority of our sample via a local health centre, where staff identified many families with children of the appropriate ages on the practice lists. However, the general practitioners (GPs) and the practice manager were clear that they would need to obtain parents' consent 'prior' to being contacted by us. The practice staff sent out letters explaining the study with tear-off slips to be marked 'I agree' or 'I do not agree' to being contacted; these were returned to the practice. Thus we were positioned at the end of a long chain of negotiation. Most potential participants did not reply and we were able to make contact with only a small number of patients. (Hood et al. 1996: 120)

Hood et al. also discuss similar problems when accessing schools and nurseries, although our own experiences show that on the whole they are more willing than health care practitioners to act as indirect rather than direct gatekeepers. For example, one of our students wished to replicate a study relating to safer sex among older school children, and after making some minor alterations to the proposed questionnaire, the head teacher allowed the researcher to give consent forms to children to give to their parents, and to the children themselves. In this way the researcher, in liaison with the school, was able to give the information she wanted in the way she wanted, rather than yet another letter from the school arriving along with the consent form for the next school outing!

Gatekeepers to children themselves, particularly when research is taking place with younger children or if it involves visiting the home environment or if it requires that children visit a special site, are the parents. If research involving children is to be successful then it is of prime importance that the relationship with parents is good. Fundamental to this process is gaining trust, which requires that you are honest, reliable and communicate well. Obvious features to maintaining a good relationship include such things as good manners – remembering to say a simple thank you may help to ensure that the parents turn up the next time.

Practical ethics involving children

It is not our intention to provide a prescriptive or restrictive approach to ethics in research involving children. Indeed it would be very difficult in any case because of the varied research approaches taken and the almost infinite research problems which could be studied. Ethics should be placed within the context of both the problem and the approach and should not be seen as an 'add-on'. It can appear sometimes in student dissertations that the same rather repetitive statements are made about informed consent, anonymity and confidentiality. The statements are without context and therefore fail to convince the reader that the researcher has thought through the ethical implications of *this* study as opposed to any other study. That is not to say that informed consent, anonymity and confidentiality are not important, because clearly they are. It is about ensuring that ethical principles are applied, which means examining the ethical implications of your study and ensuring that ethical principles are upheld in the context of your particular piece of research.

Practically, to this end, there are a number of questions which you can ask yourself as a researcher and which you can prepare answers to. There are many benefits of doing this, particularly, for example, if you are asked to attend an ethics committee hearing. The list of questions below, which we have divided into sections relating to the research process, is not finite but is designed to help you to focus on what can be a difficult task. It is also designed to reinforce the notion that ethics is not something the researcher should pay lip service to, but is of the utmost importance in any research study.

Problem

Have any ethical difficulties been raised in any of the literature relating to the research problem? If so, what were these difficulties and how were they addressed? In your opinion were they addressed in a satisfactory way? If so, why? If not, why not and what could you do to provide a satisfactory solution?

Research questions

Are your research questions necessary and of substance? Have the questions been answered before? If so, why are you doing the research? Do the questions require the involvement of child subjects? Is the involvement direct or indirect (indirect might, for example, be when research is being undertaken on another family member, or in a school)? Is it necessary to involve the child or children or can your questions be answered *by proxy*? If not, why not?

Sampling

Why have you selected the particular sampling strategy? Will your subjects understand the strategy (children can be hurt by virtue of being excluded!)? When do you intend to approach your sample? What gate-keepers do you need to contact to gain permission? Have you got permission? Do you have relevant information about your study in an appropriate format to give to your sample? How will you document their informed consent? Whom do you need to gain informed consent from? Have you done so? If the child is under 16 years old how will you demonstrate that their consent was based on understanding? Is your research therapeutic or non-therapeutic? Are there any implications relating to this?

Data collection instruments

What do your subjects need to do in order to provide you with your data? Are there any potential physical, psychological, social or emotional risks to the subjects or those close to the subject? If so are these negligible or more than negligible? How have you defined negligible? If they are more than negligible how can they be justified? If so, why? Have you explored every possible avenue to reduce risk? If not, why not? Have you checked this out with an objective third party?

Data analysis and afterwards

How have you ensured the ethical processing of data? Where will you store data? Would you be happy for such data about yourself to be stored in this way? If no, what will you do to address this? Are you breaking any data protection laws? If yes, how will you change things to ensure that you are not breaking the law? Do you break any promises or assurances made to your subjects? If yes, why? What will happen to your data after your study has been completed?

Finally, can you categorically state that, after answering all of these questions, you will do no harm to your subjects?

A concluding note

We hope by now that you will have gained an understanding that ethics is not a part of the research process that can be dismissed without thought. The ethical implications of a particular study constitute an essential consideration which is of the utmost importance. Any researcher who does not give due consideration is not only doing potential harm to the research subjects but is also potentially damaging his or her chosen profession and fellow professionals. We know of an example where one practitioner undertook research which did not adhere to ethical principles and the researcher had not gained consent from the appropriate gatekeepers. Not only were some of the research subjects extremely distressed about information given to them, all research activity (including that which had been through the appropriate access processes) was ceased, leading to a great deal of distress for colleagues.

Giving appropriate thought to potential ethical dilemmas and approaching and gaining permission from relevant gatekeepers is essential before you start to collect data. Your responsibility as an ethical researcher does not, however, cease when all permissions have been granted and consent forms signed. It continues throughout the study and extends beyond. If you are party to information which is confidential at the time of its being given it must remain confidential, and if you have made promises to destroy data you must do so.

Ethics is a very serious business, and ignoring ethics can harm your subjects, your colleagues and ultimately your own reputation as a professional and a researcher.

Practical 8.1

1 Go to the library and find out what national and international codes exist which relate directly to your own actual or potential professional grouping.
2 Write down what the code or codes say about autonomy, beneficence and justice. Does the code make specific reference to research involving children.
3 Next find a piece of research undertaken by a professional from your field which involves children. Using the code or codes you have found, and the list of questions found in the section under 'Practical ethics involving children', write down the strengths and weaknesses of the piece of research from an ethical perspective.

9 Themes and perspectives

This book has brought together research knowledge which it is intended will help to skill the professional working with children to be able to intelligently use research and to help prepare the would-be researcher by focusing on the special nature of children and research on children. We felt that this book was necessary, partly through our own observation when working with students who are preparing to work with children, and partly through our own experiences of doing research. Research texts which are generic tend to pay very little attention to the differences between undertaking research on children and undertaking research on adults – there may perhaps be a couple of lines or a paragraph given over to the special nature of children, but generally there is little if nothing at all. So the idea of the textbook was born.

What we have attempted to do is to draw out those aspects of undertaking research involving children which are different, such as special techniques and ethical implications. In other chapters we have taken generic aspects and applied them to children's settings so that the reader can grasp that all research must be contextualised. We will consider this more fully later on.

What has become apparent, however, through the writing of the book is that there are a number of common themes and perspectives which recur within each chapter and which are worthy of emphasis as we draw together what we hope you will find an exciting and meaningful text.

Children are different

At the very beginning of this book we discussed the special place which children hold in our society. They are not little adults but are developing and growing beings who have their own specific characteristics. The growing number of professional programmes which focus specifically on children emphasise the fact that working with children requires a different and distinct set of skills. This is also true of research involving children. The techniques which are required to gather data, the ethical considerations and the underpinning theories are different from those involved in researching with adult subjects. Children perceive and understand the world in a different way from adults and whilst the researcher cannot, for very obvious reasons, see the world from the child's perspective, acknowledging that their worlds are different is a sound starting point.

It is important to realise too that children do not represent an homogeneous group. Within the overarching phase of childhood there exist a multitude of differences – differences which can be as a result of age, gender, ethnicity and culture, education, social class, upbringing and so on. The list is indeed endless. We hope that, after reading our book, you have an understanding of the importance of the differences which exist between child and adult and between child and child and some of the factors which contribute to those differences.

Knowledge is the key to success

Our second theme, which clearly relates strongly to the first, is that the successful researcher undertaking research involving children must not only be aware that children are different but must also have an underlying knowledge of the child from a number of perspectives. These include knowledge of theories of emotion and cognition, of learning and personality, of physical growth and development, and of children's relationships. Apart from these basic skills the would-be researcher will also need to develop special skills which relate to the particular problem being studied. These can be achieved through wide reading and through critical analysis of previous research undertaken in a particular field. This is important if the researcher is to develop research protocols which are sensitive and appropriate. Embracing theory is fundamental to the research process, and time taken to enhance your knowledge base is time well spent.

Knowledge is also something which we can absorb through a variety of activities, not least through our everyday practice and through the observation of others who are more skilled than ourselves. The professions have traditionally relied in part upon this type of apprenticeship system whereby the student professional will work alongside those who have more experience. The amount of knowledge and how meaningful that knowledge is to us is a very individual thing. We are certainly not sponges who will absorb knowledge purely by being in a certain environment – unfortunately! We have to observe what is going on around us, ask questions, seek clarification from the literature when we do not get satisfactory answers, and we must learn to be reflective practitioners so that each new experience is thought about, compared with our past experiences and is made sense of.

Special techniques

Imagine for a moment, the ridiculous thought of a researcher entering a neonatal unit in a hospital and attempting to interview the babies! (see Figure 9.1) We have discussed above that children are different and that the researcher should hold a knowledge base which will enable greater understanding of the differences. Hand in hand with this knowledge is the repertoire of research skills which can capture the world of the child. Interviewing babies is an extreme example of incompetence but there are many grey areas between total incompetence and total competence. In the second section of the book we have placed strong focus upon the special skills and techniques which can be used when undertaking research involving children. As with all research techniques these require practice and careful consideration. We hope that this book will help you to become both discerning and discriminating when designing research. It is not enough to 'pick off the shelf' a tool designed for adult subjects.

Figure 9.1

Undertaking research with children requires special tools just as it requires special skills. We don't pretend to have all the answers by any means but the important point to make here is that you should use your knowledge of child development, and your experiences of working with children, to inform your choices. Too often students compartmentalise their knowledge into rigid boxes which disallow the integration of their knowledge. Research involves you in utilising all your skills and learning about children, because it draws upon so many theories either directly or indirectly.

Training

Our fourth key theme, which again has clear links to those mentioned above, is training. We are aware of the difficulties of being able to observe researchers directly when they are gathering data, as this may sometimes interfere with the researcher–subject relationship. There are, however, other ways of learning: through simulation, role play, in the laboratory and so on. It is also useful when learning research skills to engage expert supervision, which is the usual arrangement for students learning research as part of an academic course. There is, we believe, also a role for supervision after you have qualified, when you are undertaking research. Your supervisor might well be a colleague or a peer, rather than someone with vast amounts of experience in undertaking research, but the advantage of this type of mentorship is that it brings a fresh and more objective perspective to what you are doing. In any case, two heads are always better than one, we are told!

There are also other informal ways of gaining training when you are undertaking research. We know from experience that even the most eminent researchers are usually more than willing to discuss their research in depth with novices and students. We have had several students who have engaged in protracted international e-mail exchanges which have enabled them to gain great insight into why a researcher took a particular decision, or why they didn't pursue a specific avenue of inquiry. We have also found that, on the whole, researchers are willing to share their ideas and even their data collection instruments so long as they have access to your results. Even if you cannot engage on such a scale, if you are undertaking a study around a particular topic which is of interest to an experienced researcher, that person is likely to be interested in what you are doing and why.

The voice of children – an ongoing debate

On a different note there has appeared throughout the book a number of different perspectives and thoughts on the actual involvement of children in research. As we said in the book we do not, and indeed cannot, resolve the argument as to whether it is right or wrong to engage children within the process of research. Part of our inability to resolve what can be seen as conflict may stem from our own different academic backgrounds and associated views which stem from our own professionalisation. We are, however, not alone in experiencing some disagreement, and in Chapter 8 we refer to the different professional points of view which exist.

In practice we should perhaps embrace such differences as these for they make us question the origins of our colleagues' views rather than ignoring them. Certainly in this era of interprofessional research and education we look forward to the challenges which these different perspectives bring. Our learning must surely be richer because these differences make us reflect upon our own point of view as well as the views of others. Perhaps the next decade will resolve the debate, because it is certain we cannot move forward with interprofessional research unless some solutions are agreed upon. That does not mean, however, that we should allow our differences to halt our progress in research terms. A spirit of co-operation, respect and trust will enable healthy collaboration to take place.

Contextualisation

Our final theme, which we hope has been emphasised again and again, is that research involving children, whether their involvement is direct or indirect, must be placed into a context. We are both experienced at supervising research, doing research and reading research and with experience comes an almost intuitive understanding of what is 'good' research and what is not. We believe the answer is contextualisation. That is the ability of the researcher to really demonstrate that the research problem, the sampling, the choice of tools, the ethics and all others aspects of the research process exist in a meaningful rather than a stagnant way. Children themselves lead complex lives, and we have already referred to the need to understand the developing child. It is also important that the researcher gains an understanding of the social child. Children are not mere recipients of their environment, but they influence what goes on within their worlds and are active in making the environment what it is. Therefore, as a researcher, whatever your professional background and research tradition, it is so important that you take an holistic approach to the study of children. Only then can you understand children and only then can you start to make sense of their worlds through that enigmatic process called research.

References

Abidin, R.R. (1983) *Parenting Stress Index Manual*. Charlottesville, VA: Paediatric Psychology Press.

Abidin, R.R. (1995) *Parenting Stress Index*, 3rd edn. Windsor: NFER-Nelson.

Achenbach, T.M. (1991) *Manual for the Child Behaviour Checklists and Profile*. Burlington, VT: University of Vermont, Department of Psychiatry.

Ainsworth M.D.S., Blehar M.C., Waters, C.C.E. and Wall, S. (1978) *Patterns of Attachment: A Psychological Study of the Strange Situation*. Hillsdale, NJ: Erlbaum.

Anthony, E.J. and Bene, E. (1976) *The Family Relations Test*. Windsor: NFER-Nelson.

Axline, V. (1964) *Dibs: In Search of Self*. Harmondsworth: Penguin.

Babbie, E. (1979) *The Practice of Social Research*, 3rd edn. Nelmot, CA: Wadsworth.

Baillargeon, R. (1987) 'Object permanence in three and a half and four and a half month old infants.' *Developmental Psychology*, 23: 655–64.

Bandura, A. (1977) *Social Learning Theory*. Englewood Cliffs, NJ: Prentice Hall.

Bandura, A. (1986) *Social Foundations of Thought and Action*. Englewood Cliffs, NJ: Prentice Hall.

Bandura, A. (1992) 'Social Cognitive Theory.' In Vasta, R. (ed.) *Six Theories of Child Development: Revised Formulations and Current Issues*. London: Jessica Kingsley. pp. 1–60

Bandura, A., Ross, D. and Ross, A. (1963) 'Imitation of film-mediated aggressive models.' *Journal of Abnormal and Social Psychology*, 66: 3–11.

Barker, W. (1990) 'Practical and ethical doubts about screening for child abuse.' *Health Visitor*, 63(1): 14–17.

Baron-Cohen, S., Leslie, A.M. and Frith, U. (1985) 'Does the autistic child have a "theory of mind"?' *Cognition*, 21: 37–46.

Barsevick, A. and Llewellyn, J. (1982) 'A comparison of the anxiety-reducing potential of two bathing techniques.' *Nursing Research*, 31 (1) 2–7.

Bartsch, K. and Wellman, H. (1989) 'Young children's attribution of action to beliefs and desires.' *Child Development*, 60: 946–64.

Bayley, N. (1969) *Manual for Bayley Scales of Infant Development*. New York: Psychological Corporation.

Bayley, N. (1993) *Bayley Scales of Infant Development: Birth to Two Years*, 2nd edn. San Antonio, TX: Psychological Corporation.

Beauchamp, T.L. and Walters, L. (1989) *Contemporary Issues in Bioethics*, 3rd edn. Belfont, CA: Wadsworth.

Bell, J. (1993) *Doing Your Research Project: A Guide for First Time Researchers in Education and Social Science*. Buckingham: Open University Press.

Berk, L.E. (1994) 'Why children talk to themselves.' *Scientific American*, November: 78–83.

Berk, L.E. and Landau, S. (1993) 'Private speech of learning disabled and normally achieving children in classroom, academic and laboratory contexts.' *Child Development*, 64: 556–71.

Bick, E. (1964) 'Infant observation in psycho-analytic training.' *International Journal of Psycho-Analysis*, 45: 558–66.

Binet, A. and Simon, T. (1916/1973) *The Development of Intelligence in Children* (Elizabeth S. Kite, trans.). New York: Arno Press.

Blehar, L. and Springfield, S. (1974) 'A behaviour rating scale for the pre-school child.' *Developmental Psychology*, 10: 601–10.

Blenkin, G.M. and Yue, N.Y.L. (1994) 'Profiling early years practitioners: some first impressions from a national survey.' *Early Years*, 8 (1): 13–22.

Bowlby, J. (1951) *Maternal Care and Mental Health*. Geneva: World Health Organisation.

Bowlby, J. (1979) *The Making and Breaking of Affectional Bonds*. London and New York: Routledge.

Bowlby, J. (1995) 'An ethological approach to research in child development.' Chapter 2 in *The Making and Breaking of Affectional Bonds*. London and New York: Routledge. pp. 25–43.

Brazelton, T.B., Nugent, J.K. and Lester, B.M. (1987) 'Neonatal behavioural assessment scale.' In Osofsky, J.D. (ed.), *Handbook of Infant Development*, 2nd edn. New York: Wiley. pp. 780–817.

Bretherton, I. and Ridgeway, D. (1990) 'Story completion tasks to assess young children's internal working models of child and parent in the attachment relationship.' In M.T. Greenberg, D. Cicchetti, and E.M. Cummings (eds), *Attachment in the Pre-school Years: Theory, Research and Intervention*. Chicago and London: The University of Chicago Press. pp. 273–308.

British Psychological Society (1991) *Code of Conduct: Ethnical Principles and Guidelines*. Leicester: BPS.

Bronfenbrenner, U. (1979) *The Ecology of Human Development*. Cambridge, MA: Harvard University Press.

Bronfenbrenner, U. (1986) 'Ecology of the family as a context for human development: research perspectives.' *Developmental Psychology*, 22: 723–42.

Bronfenbrenner, U. (1992) 'Ecological systems theory.' In Vasta, R. (ed.) *Six Theories of Child Development: Revised Formulations and Current Issues*. London: Jessica Kingsley. pp 187–249.

Browne, K. (1989) 'The health visitor's role in screening for child abuse.' *Health Visitor*, 62(9): 275–7.

Buchanan, D.R. (1994) 'Reflections on the relationship between theory and practice.' *Health Education Research: Theory and Practice*, 9(3): 273–83.

Burnard, P. (1991) 'A method of analysing interview transcripts in qualitative research.' *Nurse Education Today*, 11: 461–66.

Buskist, W. and Gerbing, D.W. (1990) *Psychology: Boundaries and Frontiers*. Glenview, IL: Scott, Foresman / Little Brown Higher Education.

CESDI (1994) *Confidential Enquiry into Stillbirths and Deaths in Infancy*. London: Maternal and Child Health Research Consortium.

Charmaz, K. (1995) 'Grounded theory.' Chapter 3 in J.A. Smith, R. Harré, and L. Van Langenhove (eds), *Rethinking Methods in Psychology*. London: Sage.

Chenitz, W.C. and Swanson, J.M. (1986) *Theory From Practice to Grounded*. Menlo Park, CA: Addison-Wesley.

Child, D. (1986) *Psychology and the Teacher*, 4th edn. London: Cassell Education.

Cohen, L. and Manion, L. (eds) (1994) *Research Methods in Education*, 4th edn. London: Routledge.

Coie, J.D., Dodge, K.A. and Coppotelli, H. (1982) 'Dimensions and types of social status: a cross age perspective.' *Developmental Psychology*, 18: 557–70.

Cole, D.A., Martin, J.M. and Powers, B. (1997) 'A competency based model of child depression: a longitudinal study of peers, parent, teacher and self evaluation.' *Journal of Child Psychology and Psychiatry*, 38(5): 505–14.

Darwin, C. (1859/1985) *The Origin of the Species or The Preservation of Favoured Races in the Struggle for Life*. London: Penguin Classics.

Denham, S.A. and Auerbach, S. (1995) 'Mother–child dialogue about emotions and pre-schoolers' emotional competence.' *Genetic, Social and General Psychology Monographs*, 121(3): 311–37.

Department of Health (1989) *The Children Act*. London: HMSO.

Department of Health (1991) *Local Research Ethic Committees: NHS Executive Guidelines*. HSG (91)5.

Department of Health (1993) *Report of the Taskforce on the Strategy for Research in Nursing, Midwifery and Health Visiting*. London: HMSO.

Dimond, B. (1996a) *The Legal Aspects of Health Care*. London: Mosby.

Dimond, B. (1996b) 'Legal issues.' In L. De Raeve (ed.), *Nursing Research: an Ethical and Legal Appraisal*. London: Baillière Tindall.

Donaldson, M. (1978) *Children's Minds*. London: Fontana.

Douglas, J.W.B. (1975) 'Early hospital admission and later disturbances of behaviour and learning.' *Developmental Medicine and Child Neurology*, 17: 456–80.

Dunn, J. (1985) *Sisters and Brothers*. Cambridge, MA: Harvard University Press.

Dunn, J. (1995) 'Children as psychologists: the later correlates of individual differences in understanding of emotions and others' minds.' *Cognition and Emotion*, 9(2/3): 187–201.

Dunn, J. (1996) 'The Emanuel Miller Memorial Lecture 1995. Children's relationships: bridging the divide between cognitive and social development.' *Journal of Child Psychology and Psychiatry*, 37(5): 507–18.

Dunn, L.M. and Dunn, L.M. (1981) *Peabody Picture Vocabulary Test Revised*. Circle Pines, MN: American Guidance Service.

Dunn, L.M., Dunn, L.M., Whetton, C. and Pintilie, D. (1982) *British Picture Vocabulary Scale*. Windsor: NFER-Nelson.

Dunn, J., Slomkowski, C. and Bearsall, L. (1994) 'Sibling relationships from the pre-school period through middle childhood and early adolescence.' *Developmental Psychology*, 30: 315–24.

Edwards, A. and Talbot, R. (1994) *The Hard Pressed Researcher: A Research Handbook for the Caring Professions*. London and New York: Longman.

Elander, J. and Rutter, M. (1996) 'An update on the status of the Rutter Parents' and Teachers' Scales.' *Child Psychology and Psychiatry*, 1(1): 31–5.

Eppel, E.M. and Eppel, M. (1966) *Adolescents and Morality: A Study of some Moral Values and Dilemmas of Working Adolescents in the Context of a Changing Climate of Opinion*. London: Routledge and Kegan Paul.

Erikson, E.H. (1963) *Childhood and Society*, 2nd edn. New York: Norton.

Erikson, E.H. (1980) *Identity and the Life Cycle*. New York: Norton.

Ersser, S. (1996) 'Ethnography in clinical situations: an ethical appraisal.' In L. De Raeve (ed.), *Nursing Research: an Ethical and Legal Appraisal*. London: Baillière Tindall.

Eysenck, H.J. (1952) 'The effects of psychotherapy: an evaluation.' *Journal of Consulting Psychology*, 16: 319–24.

Eysenck, H.J. (1964) *Crime and Personality*. London: Paladin.

Fine, G.A. and Sandstrom, K.L. (1988) *Knowing Children: Participant Observation with Minors. Qualitative Research Methods,* Vol. 15. Beverly Hills: Sage.

Flannagan, C. (1993) *Psychology Practicals Made Perfect – A Level Study Guide.* Birkenhead, Merseyside: Richard Ball.

Flavell, J.H. (1978) 'The development of knowledge about visual perception.' In C.B. Keasey (ed.), *Nebraska Symposium on Motivation,* Vol. 25. Lincoln, NB: University of Nebraska Press.

Flavell, J.H. (1985) *Cognitive Development,* 2nd edn. Englewood Cliffs, NJ: Prentice Hall.

Flavell, J.H. (1988) 'The development of children's knowledge about the mind: from cognitive connections to mental representations.' In J.W. Astington, P.L. Harris and D.R. Olson (eds), *Developing Theory of Mind.* New York: Cambridge University Press. pp. 244–67.

Fonagy, P., Redfern, S. and Charman, T. (1997) 'The relationship between belief–desire reasoning and a projective measure of attachment security (SAT).' *British Journal of Developmental Psychology,* 15: 51–61.

Fraser, A. (1984) *The Weaker Vessel: Woman's Lot in Seventeenth-Century England.* London: Methuen.

Freud, S. (1901/1976) *The Psychopathology of Everyday Life.* Pelican Freud Library (4). Harmondsworth, Middlesex: Penguin.

Freud, S. (1905/1977) *Three Essays on the Theory of Sexuality.* Pelican Freud Library (7). Harmondsworth, Middlesex: Penguin.

Freud, S. (1909/1977) *Analysis of a Phobia in a Five Year Old Boy.* Pelican Freud Library (8). Harmondsworth, Middlesex: Penguin.

Freud, S. (1923/1984) *The Ego and the Id.* Pelican Freud Library (11). Harmondsworth, Middlesex: Penguin.

Glaser, B.G. and Strauss, A.L. (1967) *The Discovery of Grounded Theory.* New York: Aldine.

Gnepp, J. (1989) 'Children's use of personal information to understand other people's feelings.' In Saarni, C. and Harris, P.L. (eds), *Children's Understanding of Emotion.* New York: Cambridge University Press. pp. 151–80.

Goldsmith, D.F. and Rogoff, B. (1995) 'Sensitivity and teaching by dysphoric and nondysphoric women in structured versus unstructured situations.' *Developmental Psychology,* 31: 388–94.

Graue, M.E. and Walsh, D.J. (1996) 'Children in context: interpreting the here and now of children's lives.' Chapter 8 in J.A. Hatch (ed.), *Qualitative Research in Early Childhood Settings.* Westport, CT and London: Praeger.

Guidubaldi, J., Cleminshaw, H.K., Perry, J.D., Nastasi, B.K. and Lightel, J. (1986) 'The role of selected family environment factors in children's post-divorce adjustment.' *Family Relations,* 35: 141–51.

Hansburg, H.G. (1972) *Adolescent Separation Anxiety.* Springfield, IL: Charles Thomas.

Harlow, H.F. (1959) 'Love in infant monkeys.' *Scientific American,* 200(6): 68–74.

Harlow, H.F. and Mears, C. (1979) *The Human Model: Primate Perspectives.* New York: Wiley.

Harlow, H.F. and Zimmerman, R. (1959) 'Affectional responses in the infant monkey.' *Science,* 130: 421–32.

Hatch, J.A. (ed.) (1995) *Qualitative Research in Early Childhood Settings.* Westport, CT and London: Praeger.

Hawthorn, P. (1974) *Nurse, I Want my Mummy!* London: Royal College of Nursing.

Hay, D.F., Zahn-Waxler, C., Cummings, M. and Iannotti, R.J. (1992) 'Young children's views about conflict with peers: a comparison of the daughters and sons of depressed and well women.' *Journal of Child Psychology and Psychiatry*, 33 (4): 669–83.

Hek, G., Judd, M. and Moule, P. (1996) *Making Sense of Research: An Introduction for Nurses*. London: Cassell.

Henwood, K. and Pidgeon, N. (1995) 'Grounded theory and psychological research.' *The Psychologist*, March: 115–18.

Hetherington, E.M., Cox, M. and Cox, R. (1979) 'Play and social interaction in children following divorce.' *Journal of Social Issues*. 35: 26–49.

Hetherington, E.M., Cox, M. and Cox, R. (1985) Long-term effects of divorce and remarriage on the adjustment of the children. *Journal of the American Academy of Child Psychiatry*, 24: 518–30.

Hill, M., Laybourn, A. and Borland, M. (1996) 'Engaging with primary-aged children about their emotions and well-being: methodological considerations.' *Children and Society*, 10: 129–44.

HMSO (1990) *The Care of Children: Principles and Practice in Regulations and Guidance*. London: HMSO.

Hood, S., Kelley, P. and Mayall, B. (1996) 'Children as research subjects: a risky enterprise.' *Children and Society*, 10: 117–28.

House of Lords (1994) *Report of the Select Committee on Medical Ethics: Volume 1*. London: HMSO.

Howe, D. (1987) *An Introduction to Social Work Theory: Community Care Practice Handbook*. England: Wildwood House.

Husson, R.N., Comeau, A. and Hoff, R. (1990) Diagnosis of human immunodeficiency virus in infants and children. *Pediatrics*, 86(1): 1–9.

International Committee of the Red Cross (1949) *The Geneva Contentions of 12 August 1949*. Geneva: International Committee of the Red Cross.

Katz, J. (1992) 'Abuse of human beings for the sake of science.' In A.L. Caplan (ed.), *When Medicine Went Mad: Bioethics and the Holocaust*. Totowa, NJ: Humana Press.

Klagsbrun, M. and Bowlby, J. (1976) 'Repsonses to separation from parents: a clinical test for young children.' *British Journal of Projective Psychology and Personality Study*, 21: 7–26.

Kor, E.M. (1992) 'Nazi experiments as viewed by a survivor of Mengele's experiments.' In A.L. Caplan, (ed.), *When Medicine Went Mad: Bioethics and the Holocaust*. Totowa, NJ: Humana Press.

Kovacs, M. (1981) 'Rating scales to assess depression in school-aged children.' *Acta Paedopsychiatria*, 46: 305–15.

Kovacs, M. (1985) 'The children's depression inventory (CDI).' *Psychopharmacology Bulletin*, 21: 995–8.

Kozulin, A. (1986) 'The concept of activity in Soviet psychology: Vygotsky, his disciples and critics.' *American Psychologist*, 41 (3): 264–74.

Kulka, R.A. and Weingarten, H. (1979) 'The long-term effects of parental divorce in childhood on adult adjustment.' *Journal of Social Issues*, 35: 50–78.

Leavitt, R.L. (1996) 'The emotional culture of infant–toddler day care.' Chapter 1 in J.A. Hatch (ed.), *Qualitative Research in Early Childhood Settings*. Westport, CT and London: Praeger.

Locke, L.F., Spirduso, W.W. and Silverman, S.J. (1993) *Proposals that Work: A Guide for Planning Dissertations and Grant Proposals*. London: Sage.

Masten, A.S., Morison, P. and Pelligrini, D.S. (1985) 'A revised class play method of peer assessment.' *Developmental Psychology*, 21: 523–33.

McCall, R. B. (1994) 'Commentary.' *Human Development*, 37: 293–8.

McGuire, J. and Richman, N. (1987) *Preschool Behaviour Checklist*. Windsor: NFER-Nelson.

Mead, M. and Wolfenstein, J. (1955) *Childhood in Contemporary Cultures*. Chicago: University of Chicago Press.

Meins, E. and Russell, J. (1997) 'Security and symbolic play: the relation between security of attachment and executive capacity.' *British Journal of Developmental Psychology*, 15: 63–76.

Morrow, V. and Richards, M. (1996) 'The ethics of social research with children: an overview.' *Children and Society'* 10: 90–105.

Morse, M. (1965) *The Unattached*. Harmondsworth, Middlesex: Penguin.

Müller-Hill, B. (1992) 'Eugenics: the science and religion of the Nazis.' In A.L. Caplan (ed.), *When Medicine Went Mad: Bioethics and the Holocaust*. Totowa, NJ: Humana Press.

Murray, E.R. and Brown Smith, H. (1922) *The Child Under Eight*. London: Edward Arnold.

National Children's Bureau (1993) *Guidelines for Research*. London: NCB.

Newcombe, A.F. and Bukowski, W.M. (1984) 'A longitudinal study of the utility of social preference and social impact sociometric classification schemes.' *Child Development*, 55: 1434–47.

Newson, J. and Newson, E. (1963) *Patterns of Infant Care in an Urban Community*. Harmondsworth, Middlesex: Penguin.

Novak, M.A. and Harlow, H.F. (1975) 'Social recovery of monkeys isolated for the first year of life, 1: rehabilitation and therapy.' *Developmental Psychology*, 11: 453–65.

Oppenheim, A.N. (1966) *Questionnaire Design and Attitude Measurement*. Oxford: Heinemann.

Panton, J.H. (1945) *Modern Teaching Practice and Technique*. London: Longmans, Grenn and Co.

Pavlov, I.P. (1927) *Conditioned Reflexes*. Oxford: Oxford University Press.

Piaget, J. (1936/1952) *The Child's Conception of the World*. New York: International University Press.

Piaget, J. (1937/1954) *The Construction of Reality in the Child*. New York: Basic.

Piaget, J. (1945/1962) *Play, Dreams and Imitation in Childhood*. New York: W.W. Norton.

Pickering, N. (1996) 'Ethical review of nursing research.' In L. De Raeve (ed.), *Nursing Research: An Ethical and Legal Appraisal*. London: Baillière Tindall.

Prose, N. (1990) 'HIV infection in children.' *Journal of the American Academy of Dermatology*, 22: 1223–31.

Pugh, G; De'Ath, E. and Smith, C. (1994) *Confident Parents, Confident Children*. London: National Children's Bureau.

Radziszewska, B. and Rogoff, B. (1988) 'Influence of adult and peer collaborators in children's planning skills.' *Developmental Psychology*, 24: 840–8.

Reder, P. and Lucey, C. (1995) *Assessment of Parenting*. London: Routledge.

Reid, S. (1997) *Developments in Infant Observation: The Tavistock Model*. London and New York: Routledge.

Richman, N. and Graham, P. J. (1971) 'A behavioural screening questionnaire for use with three year old children: preliminary findings.' *Journal of Child Psychology and Psychiatry*, 12: 5–33.

Robertson, J. and Robertson, J. (1989) *Separation and the Very Young*. London: Free Association Books.

Rubin, K.H., LeMare, L.J. and Lollis, S. (1990) 'Social withdrawal in childhood: developmental pathways to peer rejection.' In S.R. Asher and J.D. Coie (eds), *Peer Rejection in Childhood*. New York: Cambridge University Press. pp. 217–49.

Rutter, M., Graham, P., Chadwick, O. and Yule, W. (1976) 'Adolescent turmoil: fact or fiction?' *Journal of Child Psychology and Psychiatry*, 17: 35–6.

Rutter, M. et al. (1979) *Fifteen Thousand Hours: Secondary Schools and their Effects on Children*. London: Open Books.

Salkind, N.J. (1985) *Theories of Human Development*, 2nd edn. Canada and Chichester: Wiley.

Samuel, J. and Bryant, P. (1984) 'Asking only one question in the conversation experiment.' *Journal of Child Psychology and Psychiatry*, 25(2): 315–18.

Schaffer, H.R. (1990) *Making Decisions about Children: Psychological Questions and Answers*. Oxford: Blackwell.

Schaffer, H.R. and Emmerson, P.E. (1964) 'The developments of social attachment in infants.' *Monographs of the Society for Research in Child Development*, 29 (3, Serial number 94).

Segal, N.L. (1992) 'Twin research at Auschwitz-Birkenau.' In A.L. Caplan (ed.), *When Medicine Went Mad: Bioethics and the Holocaust*. Totowa, NJ: Humana Press.

Seidman, I. (1998) *Interviewing As Qualitative Research: A Guide For Researchers In Education and the Social Services*. New York: Teachers College Press.

Sheridan, M.D. (1975) *From Birth to Five Years: Children's Developmental Progress*, 3rd edn. Windsor: NFER.

Silverman, D. (ed.) (1996) *Qualitative Research*. London: Sage.

Siperstein, G.N. (1979) 'A scale for measuring attitudes toward mildly and severely mentally retarded persons.' Unpublished manuscript, University of Massachusetts, Boston.

Skinner, B.F. (1938) *The Behavior of Organisms*. New York: Appleton-Century Croft.

Skinner, B.F. (1974) *About Behaviourism*. New York: Vintage.

Spangler, G. and Grossman, K.E. (1993) 'Biobehavioural organisation in securely and insecurely attached infants.' *Child Development*, 64: 1439–50.

Stern, D. (1977) *The First Relationship: Infant and Mother*. London: Fontana/Open Books.

Stern, P.N. (1985) 'Using grounded theory method in nursing research.' In M.M. Leininger (ed.), *Qualitative Research Methods in Nursing*. Orlando, FL: Grune and Stratton.

Stine, G.J. (1997) *AIDS Update 1997: An Annual Overview of Acquired Immune Deficiency Syndrome*. Upper Saddle River, NJ: Prentice Hall.

Storr, A. (1964) *Sexual Deviation*. Harmondsworth, Middlesex: Penguin.

Sylva, K., Roy, C. and Painter, M. (1980) *Childwatching at Playgroup and Nursery School: Oxford Pre-School Project Grant*. London: McIntyre.

Taylor, J. (1996) 'Health promotion.' In McQuaid, L., Huband, S. and Parker, E. (eds), *Children's Nursing*. Edinburgh: Churchill Livingstone.

Taylor, J. (1997) 'Children in developing countries.' Chapter 13 in J. Taylor and M. Woods (eds), *Early Childhood Studies: an Holistic Introduction*. London: Arnold.

Taylor, J. and Müller, D. (1995) *Nursing Adolescents: Research and Psychological Perspectives.* Oxford: Blackwell Scientific.

Taylor, J. and Woods, M. (eds) (1997) *Early Childhood Studies: An Holistic Approach.* London: Arnold.

Tizard, B. and Hodges, J. (1978) 'The effect of early institutional rearing on the development of eight year old children.' *Journal of Child Psychology and Psychiatry,* 19: 99–118.

Tizard, B. and Rees, J. (1975) 'The effect of early institutional rearing on the behaviour and affectional relationships of four year old children.' *Journal of Child Psychology and Psychiatry,* 16: 61–73.

Trowell, J. and Miles, G. (1996) 'The contribution of observation training to professional development in social work.' In G. Bridge and G. Miles, *On the Outside Edge Looking In: Collected Essays on Young Child Observation in Social Work Training.* London: CCETSW.

UNICEF (1989) *Universal Declaration of the Rights of the Child.* New York: UNICEF.

Vigorito, S.S. (1992) 'A profile of Nazi medicine.' In A.L. Caplan (ed.), *When Medicine Went Mad: Bioethics and the Holocaust.* Totowa, NJ: Humana Press.

Vygotsky, L.S. (1978) *Mind in Society: The Development of Higher Mental Processes.* Cambridge, MA: Harvard University Press.

Wattley, L.A. and Müller, D.J. (1984) *Investigating Psychology: A Practical Approach for Nursing.* London: Harper and Row.

Watson, J.B. (1930) *Behaviourism.* New York: W.W. Norton.

Wechsler, D. (1974) *Wechsler Intelligence Scale For Children.* New York: Psychological Corporation.

Wechsler, D. (1989) *Wechsler Pre-School and Primary Scale of Intelligence Revised.* San Antonio, TX: The Psychological Corporation.

Wechsler, D. (1991) *Manual for the Wechsler Intelligence Scale for Children III.* San Antonio, TX: The Psychological Corporation.

Wertsch, J.V. (1979) 'From social interaction to higher psychological processes: a clarification and application of Vygotsky's theory.' *Human Development,* 22: 1–22.

Wertsch, J.V. and Hickman, M. (1987) 'Problem solving in social interaction: a microgenetic analysis.' In M. Hickman (ed.), *Social and Functional Approaches to Language and Thought.* New York: Academic Press. pp. 251–66.

Whiting, B. (1963) *Six Cultures: Studies of Child Rearing.* New York: Wiley.

Whiting, B. and Edwards, C. (1988) *Children of Different Worlds.* Cambridge, MA: Harvard University Press.

Whiting, B. and Whiting, J. (1975) *Children of 6 Cultures.* Cambridge, MA: Harvard University Press.

Woods, M. (1997) 'Early childhood education in pre-school settings.' In Taylor, J. and Woods, M. (eds), *Early Childhood Studies: An Holistic Approach.* London: Arnold.

World Health Organisation (1951) *Expert Committee on Mental Health, Report on the Second Session 1951.* Technical Report Series No. 31. Geneva: WHO.

Yin, R.K. (1994) *Case Study Research Design and Methods,* 2nd edn. Thousand Oaks: Sage.

Recommended further reading

Chapter 2

Dunn, J. (1994) 'Understanding others and the social world: current issues in developmental research and their relation to pre-school experiences and practice.' *Journal of Applied Developmental Psychology*, 15: 571–83.

Dunn, J. and Brown, J. (1994) 'Affect expression in the family, children's understanding of emotions and their interactions with others.' *Merrill-Palmer Quarterly*, 40(1): 120–37.

Gibbons, J. (ed.) (1992) *The Children Act 1989 and Family Support: Principles into Practice*. London: HMSO.

Greig, A.D. (1997) 'Play, language and learning.' Chapter 9 in J. Taylor and M. Woods (eds), *Early Childhood Studies: An Holistic Approach*. London: Arnold.

Howe, D. (1996) *Attachment Theory for Social Work Practice*. Macmillan: London.

Lindon, J. (1996) *Growing Up: From Eight Years to Young Adulthood*. London: National Children's Bureau.

Müller, D.J., Harris, P.J., Wattley, L. and Taylor, J.D. (1992) *Nursing Children: Psychology, Research and Practice*, 2nd edn. London: Chapman and Hall.

Rutter, M. and Hay, D.F. (eds) (1994) *Development Through Life: A Handbook for Clinicians*. Oxford: Blackwell Scientific.

Schaffer, H.R. (1996) *Social Development*. Oxford: Blackwell.

Taylor, J. and Woods, M. (eds) (1997) *Early Childhood Studies: An Holistic Approach*. London: Arnold.

Vasta, R. (ed.) (1992) *Six Theories of Child Development: Revised Formulations and Current Issues*. London: Jessica Kingsley.

Wood, D. (1994) *How Children Think and Learn*. Oxford: Blackwell.

Chapter 3

Gillet, G. (1995) 'The philosophical foundations of qualitative psychology.' *The Psychologist*, March: 111–14.

Henwood, K. and Nicolson, P. (1995) 'Qualitative research.' *The Psychologist*, March: 109–10.

Pugh, G. (1996) *Children and Society: Special Issue*, 10.

Sherrard, C. (1997) 'Qualitative research: never mind the bath water, keep hold of the baby!' *The Psychologist*, October: 161–2.

Smith, J.A. (1995) 'Qualitative methods, identity and transition to motherhood.' *The Psychologist*, March: 122–5.

Stevenson, C. and Cooper, N. (1997) 'Qualitative and Quantitative Research.' *The Psychologist*, October: 159–60.

Tizard, I.B. (1990) 'Research and policy: is there a link?' *The Psychologist*, October: 435–40.

Wertsch, J.V. and Tulviste, P. (1992) 'L.S. Vygotsky and contemporary developmental psychology.' *Developmental Psychology*, 28: 548–57.

Chapter 7

Buchsbaum, H., Toth, S.L., Clyman, R.B., Cicchetti, D. and Emde, R.N. (1992) 'The use of a narrative story stem technique with maltreated children: implications for theory and practice.' *Development and Psychopathology*, 4: 603–25.

George, C. (1996) 'A representational perspective of child abuse and prevention: internal working models of attachment and caregiving.' *Child Abuse and Neglect*, 20(5): 411–424.

Index